For Keith, Angel and Tashi, with love

© Jessie Kirkness Parker

First Published 2006 by Jerboa Books
Second Edition 2008 by Turath, an imprint of Jerboa Books
PO BOX 333838 Dubai UAE
www.jerboabooks.com
ISBN 9948-431-13-8

Approved by the National Information Council UAE:
No 711 9 May 2006

Food Photography by Trevor Vaughan

A Taste of Arabia

Jessie Kirkness Parker

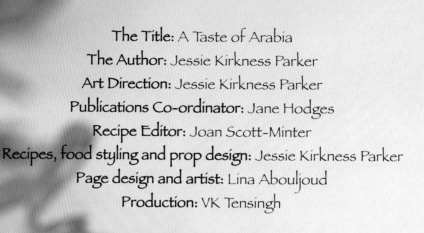

The Title: A Taste of Arabia
The Author: Jessie Kirkness Parker
Art Direction: Jessie Kirkness Parker
Publications Co-ordinator: Jane Hodges
Recipe Editor: Joan Scott-Minter
Recipes, food styling and prop design: Jessie Kirkness Parker
Page design and artist: Lina Aboujloud
Production: VK Tensingh

Text and photography © Jessie Kirkness Parker
Design and Layout © Jerboa Books

Printed in Dubai

Contents

Foreword

There is a splash of water and hands are washed. 'Bismillah', praise be to God, the meal begins. Undaunted and unconquered by some of the greatest desert sands in the world, these recipes are my personal view of Arabia's robust cuisines. They are a tribute to this region's inventiveness, a triumph of delicious flavours, and in praise of gentle customs. I am passionate about the flavours in Arabia. Year-round sunshine plus centuries of exploration in the use of spices inject these down-to-earth, ethnic recipes with energy, respect for simple ingredients, and joy of cooking.

The mysteries of the region's flavours are locked into a unique Arabic spice mixture called *biz'har*. Generally, homemakers guard the intricacies of their family *biz'har* recipe. Secreted into it is the exotic flavour of dried lime, called *loomi* with its souring qualities of both lemon peel and the bracing freshness of a spritz of lime.

Traditional recipes are variable and innumerable - and so they should be. I believe recipes are meant to be a personal expression. Many of the recipes in this book are fragrant one-pot glories or simple, brilliant barbecues to make your own. Use the quantities suggested as guidelines only. For example, if you like strong pungent flavours, add a little more chilli to your *biz'har* or use any of the milder versions or marinades. Leave out cardamom if you loathe it, or add a little more cumin if you love it. Nobody can tell you exactly how to season or present your dishes. Large portions of rice are the mainstay of much of the Arab world's diet, while in the West, smaller portions are usual.

While ready-made *biz'har* can be store bought, gathering spices to make your first home-made *biz'har* should be intriguing. Unless you already have one, I urge you to buy your first pestle and mortar. To bash and bruise the world's barks, seeds and pods, and to unlock the flavours, colours and aromas of the Middle East is to experience the most amazing and best of culinary journeys!

Wishing you the best of happy cooking and *sa'ha'tian*, bon appetit!

Jessie

A sardine shoal breaks the surface at dawn
Ras Al Khaimah harbour 1978

All photographs of the Emirates are by the
author and her husband, Keith.

5

Flavours

biz'har and loomi

Biz'har or Arabic masalas are unique spice mixtures or *baharat*. These flavour many of the recipes in A Taste of Arabia, with the lemon and lime qualities of dried limes, called *loomi*.

easy pan-roasted powdered biz'har

* 1/2 teaspoon powdered turmeric
* 3 teaspoons powdered paprika
* 2 teaspoons powdered black peppercorns
* 4 teaspoons powdered cumin seeds
* 1 teaspoon grated nutmeg
* 1 1/2 teaspoons powdered coriander seeds

* 1-2 teaspoons powdered cardamom pods
* 1 teaspoon powdered cinnamon bark
* 1 teaspoon dried powdered red Kashmiri chilli
* 1 powdered clove
* 1 powdered *loomi* (optional)

Mix all the ingredients together in a non-stick pan. Dry-roast, stirring continuously for 1 minute or until aromas perfume the air. Turn out onto a flexible chopping board or a stiff piece of smooth, clean paper to cool for 3 minutes, then pour them into a coffee grinder or similar. Grind to a powder; seal in an airtight container and store on a dark shelf or, when cool, store in the fridge; use within 3 months. For outstanding results, select whole spices instead of powdered ones, and dry-roast as above. Experiment with various spice mixture variations by adding dried fennel seeds for fish dishes or grated nutmeg for chicken and vegetable dishes. For a milder version omit the chilli. **Makes 25g or 2 1/2 tablespoons.**

Biz'har, Arabic spice mixture, does vary from home to home and, in my recipes, loomi (*pictured below and foreground, page 9*) are nearly always popped into the poaching liquid then stewed or steamed and not mixed into the *biz'har*. This way, their dark colouring stays mostly in the fruit.

biz'har
broad beans
cardamom
chickpeas
cinnamon

Biz'har SUBSTITUTE
Curry powder may be used instead of *biz'har* in all the recipes throughout the book, or ready made Arabic Masala can be bought.

Loomi SUBSTITUTE
If *loomi* is unavailable omit from the *biz'har* and replace each *loomi* with grams lemon peel and the juice of 1 lime.

cloves
coriander
cumin
date syrup
dates

All the spices can be found in stores specialising in Middle Eastern foodstuffs.
You can dry your own limes in the oven at a low temperature overnight or see substitute above.

dill
freekeh
garlic
ginger
herbed tea
honey

7

coffee

Home-made Arabic coffee or *gah'wa* is deliciously spicy with fantastic aromas.

Make it unsweetened and cardamom-scented as is done in the Gulf; it is massively revitalising. A typical Gulf serving is traditionally poured from an Arabic coffee pot into cone-shaped, tiny coffee cups, *finj'aan*, pictured on page 104. One serving would fill an espresso cup only to one third full but expect to accept a few refills before giving the *finj'aan* a little jiggle to indicate that you want no more. Do not be surprised if, to save precious water in remote areas, your *finj'aan* enjoys only a brief communal wash in a small basin of detergent-free water, along with the other cups, before the host or hostess shakes it off and offers it to the next guest.

Coffee, Gah'wa: place 1 tablespoon or 8 grams of roasted coffee beans and 2 cardamom pods in a coffee grinder and grind until fine; transfer to a small, long handled coffee pot or pan. Pour in one scant cup or 200 ml of pure cool or fresh filtered water. I was taught to make it ritually: bring it up to boiling point and then let it settle; repeat three times. Finally, let it settle and serve by carefully pouring the coffee off the top into the *finj'aan*. For the spicy version: place a pinch of saffron and a pinch of cloves in a vacuum flask; pour in brewed coffee as described above. **Both recipes serve 4; reckon on three Gulf-size servings or a scant quarter cup per serving.**

cha'i

During the holy month of *Ramadan*, tea frequently breaks the fast along with dates. Green is the colour of sanctity so I like making Arabic herbed teas in green cups, *ista'akan*, or in hand-painted Moroccan glasses.

Za'atar tea, *Cha'i Za'atar*: when infused into green or black teas, it is delectable. Pour some boiling water into a 2 cup or 500 ml teapot; swirl it round to rinse and warm the pot; drain. Place 2 sprigs of *za'atar* and 1-2 tablespoons of tea leaves into the teapot; pour on boiling water and leave to infuse for 3 minutes.

Mint tea, Cha'i nah'na: make as above using around 20 large mint leaves instead of fresh *za'atar* leaves; it may be sweetened with sugar directly in the pot.

Herb and fruit tree gardens are cosseted in date palm oases, some of which are still *falaj*-fed with precious sweet water in remote desert areas.

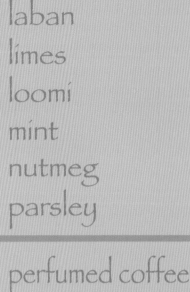

laban
limes
loomi
mint
nutmeg
parsley

Souqs are stacked with sacks piled high with mature basmati and pearls of Egyptian rice. Canopied spice *souqs* are crammed with pyramids of spices, dried limes, *loomi*, rose petals, saffron and wild thyme, *za'atar*. Importantly, they house mill shops where spices are freshly ground on demand.

perfumed coffee
red onions
rocca
rose syrup
saffron

sea salt and freshly ground black pepper
Sprinkle sea salt and ground black or white pepper throughout the making of a dish. Instead of tasting harsh pepper and salt flavours, resulting from one single seasoning blast at the end of cooking, this method constructs a natural flavour boost of each of the ingredients' character as they cook.

sesame seeds
sumac
tahina
watercress
white radish
za'atar

lime and cumin-scented chickpeas and broad beans

These were Bedouin enchantments when I first tasted them one afternoon, in a hill village home near Hatta in the Hajar Mountains, and I still rate them as a great snack, healthful and brimming with delicious flavour. Makes 3 cups of each; offer them as snacks with *za'atar*, mint flavoured tea or cardamom-infused coffee.

* 250g dried chickpeas
* 250g dried broad beans
* 4 tablespoons cumin powder
* 2 large peeled and quartered potatoes
* 4 large peeled and quartered red onions
* 2 bay leaves
* 2 star anise
* 8 black peppercorns
* a few stalks and leaves of parsley
* a few stalks and leaves of coriander
* sea salt
* 2 *loomi*
* juice of 4 limes
* approximately 4-5 litres water

1 Soak the chickpeas and broad beans overnight in separate, very large, deep bowls of fresh, room temperature water. Make sure there is plenty of water to cover as the peas and beans will absorb roughly two or three times their volume.

2 Drain the chickpeas and beans and put into two separate saucepans.

3 Divide the rest of the ingredients, except *loomi* and lime juice, equally between the pans making sure that the water covers them by 1 centimetre. Boil, partially covered, for 1 hour or until tender. Ten minutes before the end of the cooking time, add one tablespoonful of sea salt, the *loomi* and lime juice to each of the pans.

4 Taste the peas and beans checking for tenderness and flavour; if necessary cook longer and add salt to taste. Drain and cool slightly; discard the herbs and vegetables. Serve separately with a small bowl of cumin powder and another of freshly cut lime halves.

Bedouin enchantments

The first thing I noticed was the precision with which the limes and other fruit had been cut and laid out on a large, round metal tray, *fu'alla*. Sliced down on either side of the stalk and pith were fat, small, lime belly halves ready for easy pip-free squeezing over food.

My hosts demonstrated first, with an expression of gratitude, the devotional *'al'hum'dul'leela,'* and then I followed, spritzing lime halves and dusting cumin over the chickpeas, *dango*, and broad beans, *barjilla*. Their flavours were astonishingly addictive.

I also serve a small jug of freshly squeezed lime juice, pre-mixed with cumin, to pour over the peas and beans from time to time to keep them moist.

For concentrated flavour, I like to cook the chickpeas and broad beans first in highly flavoured cumin and *loomi* vegetable stock.

za'atar, pictured pages 2-3

Intensely tangy thyme zest lies within its olive-green, delicate, oregano-like leaves.

Za'atar, a herb that is part of the family *Thymus vulgare*, makes an aromatic, powerful contribution to the Gulf and eastern Mediterranean cuisines. It is referred to variously as Arabic thyme, wild marjoram or 'Greek oregano'. *Za'atar's* spice mixture passionately infuses and enriches these cuisines. Its mixture of crunchy sesame seeds, lemony *sumac*, salt and zesty *za'atar* seasons croissants, spices bread doughs and perks up *falafel*. For breakfast or snacks with tea, it might be mixed with white cream cheese or olive oil and smeared over Arabic flat breads, *cho'bab*, or toasted baguettes.

ginger-spiked laban, pictured page 10

Pouring quickly and slightly thicker than milk into my glass, the first drinking yogurt or Arabic *laban* I ever tasted was ice-chilled, tart, balanced with salt, and flashy with a jolt of green chilli - a deeply satisfying, thirst quenching experience, sweetly remembered.

That one was home-made, a yogurt made from culturing goat's milk. Now I buy ready-made cow's milk *laban* and I have since learnt to make it flavoured with a variety of herbs and spices: dried mint or fenugreek, cardamom or saffron but my favourite by far is with finely grated fresh ginger root and sea salt. Elsewhere, as a substitute for Arabic *laban*, buy cultured buttermilk or drinking yogurt and dilute three parts of it with one part mineral water to mimic *laban's* unique tart, not sour, flavour.
See SERVING, page 25.

Pour 4 cups or 1 litre of ice-cold *laban* into a large jug; add 4 tablespoons peeled and finely grated fresh ginger root, 1 1/2 teaspoons sea salt, 1/2 or 1 whole slit and seeded green chilli (optional) and 1 cup of ice cubes. Blend well. **Makes one litre; serve in 6 small, Moroccan decorative glasses.**

mint & lime soda, pictured opposite

Whizz the juice of 350g limes (1/2 cup) and 2 lemons (1/2 cup); 2 cups ice cubes; 4 cups (50g) loosely packed mint leaves; 2 cans diet lemonade soda or 3 cups soda and sugar syrup to taste. **Makes 1 litre.**

Rice

lamb kaab'sa

I have always loved lamb with fruits and nuts. Showered with roasted pine nuts and almonds, plump sultanas and spritzed with tangy lime, this pilaf has tender lamb morsels falling off the bone, cooked in an aromatic yogurt-enriched lamb stock.

Served at banquets and everyday lunch, I like it rich with a generous amount of lamb and extra quantities of my ginger and garlic-infused caramelised brown onions, which are an essential garnish. **Serves 6-7 in the Middle East as a main meal and 8-10 in the West.**

* 1500g leg of lamb, well trimmed of all fat and cut into large 4 centimetre chunks
* 2 1/2 tablespoons *biz'har*, page 6
* sea salt and freshly ground black pepper
* 2-3 tablespoons, around 75 ml, olive oil or ghee
* 4 medium sliced red onions
* 2 mashed garlic cloves
* 1 centimetre peeled and grated fresh ginger root
* 5 cups lamb stock, pages 50-52
* 1 cup or 250g plain yogurt
        whole spices:
        4 cinnamon sticks
        3 bay leaves
        2 black cardamoms, optional
        8 roughly bruised, split green cardamom pods
        4 cloves
        2 loomi or the zest of one lemon

* 3 cups basmati rice
* 3 skinned, seeded and chopped tomatoes
* 2 sliced green chillies, optional
* a pinch or two of powdered saffron strands soaked in 3 tablespoons boiling water
* 2 tablespoons *ghee* or clarified butter or olive oil

* 1 cup mixture of pine nuts, almonds and pistachios
* 1 teaspoon powdered *loomi*
* 1/2 cup or 100g soft sultanas, soaked and drained

garnish:
* 2 cups yogurt, *laban* or spiked laban, page 12
* 8 limes, sliced in half

1 Rub half the *biz'har* into the lamb; season with sea salt and freshly ground black pepper and leave to rest while you prepare all the remaining ingredients.

2 Heat the olive oil in a large, heavy saucepan and then add the onions. Stir-fry on a medium high heat until they are soft, transparent, and well glazed to a golden brown, around 6 minutes. Remove and drain on a paper towel, reserving half for cooking with the lamb, and the remaining half for garnish. Add the lamb and stir-fry until well browned on a high heat until the aromas of the marinade perfume the air, around 3 minutes. Reduce to a medium to low heat or the spices will burn. Add more oil if the lamb is sticking and let it brown further for another 5 minutes, then return half the onions and all the garlic and grated ginger, stirring from time to time to brown evenly without burning, another 2-3 minutes. If the pan seems too hot, add a little water to stop the spices from burning.

3 Add enough lamb stock to cover the meat by 1 centimetre, around 5 cups; however, if you like your rice moist, add 6 cups. Scrape the bottom of the pan to loosen the onions, spices and flavours into the stock. Slowly add the yogurt to the dish and let it come to a simmer slowly. Add all the whole spices. Let the meat poach in the softly simmering stock, uncovered, for 40 minutes or until tender, stirring from time to time.

4 While the meat is poaching, measure out the rice into a bowl. Gently rinse and drain twice. See HANDLING page 25. Pour into a colander or sieve and leave to drain, covered, for about 15 minutes.

5 When the meat is tender, add the tomatoes and chillies. Season the stew with 1 tablespoon sea salt to taste and stir in well. Sprinkle the drained rice over the surface of the poached lamb stew. Stir just once very gently or the rice grains will break. Simmer, covered, for about 10 minutes or until most of the stock has been absorbed and the rice is cooked al dente.

6 Turn off the heat and sprinkle the soaked saffron and its water over the surface of the *kaab'sa*. Cover tightly; let it stand for 10 minutes. Just before serving, heat the ghee or butter or olive oil in a separate non-stick pan. Add the pine nuts, almonds and pistachios, the remaining *biz'har*, soaked sultanas and powdered dried *loomi*. Serve the *kaab'sa* onto a large serving platter showered with fruit and nut mixture.

Flavoured and coloured with spices, aromatic barks and seeds, perfumed with saffron and showered with caramelised onions, fried vermicelli, nuts, fruit and herbs such as coriander, or just plain white basmati, *aish*, rice is always on the menu. Every day, steaming platters of rice are served as the centrepiece of lunch or the main meal.

During the holy month of *Ramadan*, a pilaf is ideally suited to restoring energy after fasting and cause for celebration at the *Iftar* meal, after breaking the daily fast with dates, yogurt, coffee or tea.

The focus at *Eid* celebrations is a huge family meal of favourite lamb biryani-style pilafs such as *kaab'sa*, *machboos* or *gouzi*, which is a spectacular and much fêted dish of stuffed roasted lamb with a highly seasoned pilaf in which small roast chickens nestle.

Sheikh Rashid Bin Saeed Al Maktoum, the ruler of Dubai from 1958-1990
Picture by the author

my chicken machboos

This traditional Bedouin pilaf is a one-pot wonder. It starts life as a scrumptious chicken-on-the-bone stew, submersed in glorious aromatic spicy gravy.

In this recipe, soaked basmati rice cooks and steams on the gentlest of heat for 30 minutes, absorbing the spicy chicken stock flavours, as well as retaining the reds of Kashmiri chilli powder and the golds of saffron into their plump, long elegant rice grains. Serving it is easy: turn the whole lot out onto a serving platter with nuts, coriander leaves and tangy fresh tomato chutney, see page 29, tumbling over it. Traditional garnishes of yogurt, lime halves and sliced radish add fantastic crunch and relish. But for an *Eid* feast or celebration, garnishes may include plump yellow sultanas, roasted almonds and cashew nuts. I leave the bone in because that is where the flavour lies; it may be easier to ask your butcher to 'joint the chicken for sauté'. **Serves 8 in the Middle East and 10-12 in the West.**

* 1 large chicken, skinned and cut into 10-12 pieces
     machboos marinade:
     1 teaspoon roughly crushed cumin seeds
     4 roughly crushed cloves
     2 teaspoons *biz'har*, page 6
     2 teaspoons turmeric powder
     5 cloves of grated or mashed garlic
     3 teaspoons red Kashmiri chilli powder
     juice of 2 limes
     1/4 cup or 150 ml olive oil
* sea salt and freshly ground black pepper
* 3 medium or 250g sliced red onions
* 4 medium or 400g skinned, seeded and chopped tomatoes
* 1 x 227g tinned chickpeas
* 2-3 *loomi*

whole spices:
6 cinnamon sticks
6-8 bruised, split green cardamom pods
2 bay leaves
5 peppercorns
* 5 cups or 1.25 litres chicken stock
* 3 cups or 600g basmati rice
* 2 pinches, about 1 teaspoon of powdered
   saffron strands soaked in 3 tablespoons of
   boiling water
* 4 tablespoons hot melted butter or ghee

1 Place the chicken pieces in a bowl.

2 To prepare the marinade, crush and bruise the cumin seeds and the cloves in a pestle and mortar and sprinkle over the chicken. Season lightly with a little sea salt and freshly ground black pepper; add the *biz'har*, additional turmeric powder, mashed garlic and red chilli powder. Squeeze the juice of 1 lime over the chicken pieces and rub in well. Cover and leave to stand.

3 Pour 3 tablespoons of boiling water over the powdered saffron strands and leave to soak.

4 Meanwhile, pour the olive oil into a large, roomy, heavy saucepan and stir-fry the onions on a medium to high heat until they are caramelised, very crispy and golden brown, about 10 minutes. Remove and drain on a paper towel. If necessary, add two additional tablespoons of the olive oil to the pan. Add the chicken pieces and stir-fry until golden brown, around 8-10 minutes on a medium to high heat, making sure that it does not stick and burn. Add the tomatoes, season with a little sea salt and pepper, if preferred, and add the chickpeas, *loomi*, whole spices and half the reserved onions. Stir-fry for 1 minute to coat all the ingredients with the pan's flavours.

5 Stir in the chicken stock, cover with a tightly fitting lid, and bring to a gentle simmer. Add 1 tablespoon of salt or more to taste and poach, gently simmering for 30 minutes without lifting the lid.

6 Fifteen minutes into the cooking time begin to prepare the rice: measure it into a bowl; gently rinse and drain twice, page 25. Finally, cover with fresh water and leave to soak for 15 minutes. Taste the stock, and add up to one tablespoon of sea salt to taste. Drain the rice and carefully sprinkle it over the surface of the simmering chicken stew. Do not stir. Simmer, firmly covered, for about 15 minutes or until the rice is cooked al dente.

7 Turn off the heat and sprinkle the soaked saffron with its water over the rice; do not stir in the saffron. Replace the lid firmly and for the next 15 minutes either let it stand and steam in the pan or steam it in a pre-heated hot oven (200°C).

8 To serve, flick the saffron-coloured rice with a fork to mix without breaking the rice grains. Serve from the pot or turn the whole lot out, Arab-style, onto a serving platter. Top with the remaining reserved caramelised brown onions and serve with the garnishes. Please note that the whole spices are not meant to be eaten, though a nibble on the *loomi* is delicious.

The inauguration of Jebel Ali Harbour
Dubai 1979
Picture by the author

21

stuffed baby marrows in laban

Stuffed with fat, creamy, starchy Egyptian rice, this humble vegetable is surprisingly delicious. Cooked to tenderness in a light, buttery *laban* and chicken stock, the flavours are comforting and nourishing.

I always blanch the baby marrows first; it firms them up, fixes their colour to a fresh green and reduces any chance of their high water content diluting the flavours of the dish. Pick out unblemished baby marrows; those that are firm, have good green colour, are tight-skinned and small are best. Expect to spend around 25 minutes hollowing out their centres with a vegetable corer and stuffing them; the stew takes 30 minutes to cook through in the pan. The stuffed marrows can also be cooked in the spicy tomato sauce, page 90, drizzled with extra virgin olive oil and served as a vegetable side dish or chilled snack. Serves 6, allowing three per person as a light main course and served with vermicelli rice or plain white rice. In the Gulf, they are often served as a side vegetable dish, serving 6-8 along with a rice pilaf and a stew such as *saloona*.

* 1.4 kg small-size baby marrows,
  each weighing around 120g
* sea salt and freshly ground white pepper
   stuffing:
   2 tablespoons Egyptian rice
   1/2 cup pine nuts
   2 tablespoons olive oil
   1 large finely chopped onion
   200g minced lean lamb
   3 cloves crushed garlic
   1 teaspoon *biz'har*, page 6
   1 teaspoon powdered cinnamon

* 1 tablespoon of olive oil
* 1 finely sliced onion
* 1 sliced tomato
* 2 cloves crushed garlic
* 1 teaspoon dried mint
* 1/4 cup chopped flat leaf parsley
* 4 cups yogurt or laban
* 1 cup chicken stock
* 1 tablespoon diced, ice-cold
  butter or 2 tablespoons cream

1 Soak the Egyptian rice in half a cup of warm water.

2 Wash the marrow thoroughly. Have a large bowl of fresh chilled water ready. Slice off the stalk end. Core a hollow in the centre of the marrow using an Arabic long-bladed vegetable corer, careful to ensure that the hollow reaches all the way down the length of the marrow without breaking through to the other end. Put each prepared marrow into the water while you core the rest.

3 To blanch the marrows, bring a large saucepan of fresh, salted water to the boil. Add the drained marrows and boil for 3 minutes. Before removing, check that they are slightly soft; let them boil for another minute if necessary. Scoop them out of the water using a slotted spoon and plunge them back into the bowl with the chilled water. When cool, drain and leave in a colander to drain further. Dry-roast the pine nuts in a non-stick pan until golden. Remove and place in a mixing bowl; add the drained rice. Heat the olive oil in a non-stick frying pan, add the onion and stir-fry until soft. Add all the remaining stuffing ingredients; season well with sea salt and freshly ground white pepper and mix well. Stir-fry quickly on a medium heat for 5-6 minutes. Turn out into the mixing bowl. When cool enough to handle, stuff the baby marrows. Pack the mixture in firmly, but not tightly.

4 Heat the oil to a medium heat in a large, heavy saucepan. Add the sliced onion and stir-fry for 4-5 minutes until soft, transparent and lightly browned. Add the sliced tomatoes, the flat leaf parsley, garlic and mint; stir-fry for a couple of minutes. Reduce the heat to very low, then smooth out in an even layer over the bottom of the pan.

5 Place a layer of the stuffed marrows side by side into the casserole or saucepan. Repeat in layers until they are tightly packed. Place a heat-proof plate on top to keep them in position while cooking. Mix together the chicken stock and *laban* and pour in over the plate. Cover and bring to a simmer over a gentle heat for about 10 minutes or until the marrows are cooked al dente. Lift the plate off; remove the marrows with a slotted spoon and arrange in a large, deep serving dish; keep warm.

6 Boil to reduce the remaining stock in the pan, uncovered, for about another 20 minutes to intensify the flavours. Cool slightly and blend until smooth. Just before serving, quickly hand whisk the butter (or cream), a little at a time, into the stock and pour over the marrows and serve immediately.

BUYING Most cooks in this region look at the expiry date of rice from a unique perspective. They greatly value mature rice and will lay it down for years - 10 years or more - knowing that it develops a greater capacity for absorption and flavour.

HANDLING Measure out the rice into a bowl. Cover with fresh water and gently rinse, running your fingers under water with the rice. Pour off the starch-filled water. Rinse and drain again. Cover the rice with plenty of fresh, cold water and leave to soak for 15 minutes. Finally, drain and use as directed in the recipe.

TO TEST IF DONE
Unless the recipe is for risotto, plain rice or pilaf rice is always cooked al dente, literally meaning 'to the teeth', soft and fluffy - not overcooked and mushy.

SERVING I like to turn out the rice or pilaf, Arabic-style, onto an enormous platter, serving the traditional accompaniment of yogurt or drinking yogurt, *laban*, page 12, which may be poured over the pilaf or drunk from a glass.

In addition to offering the customary garnishes of lime halves, dates, radishes, fresh *za'atar* leaves, dill and green salad in pretty bowls, I like to serve my recipe for fresh tomato chutney, page 29, or the carrot garnish, opposite, creating opportunity for ample flavour variations.

GRATED CARROT GARNISH
Heat a teaspoon of olive oil in a non-stick pan; pan-roast one chopped green chilli and a handful of cashew and pine nuts; season with sea salt and white pepper. Add two grated carrots and a quarter cup coriander leaves and mix. Shower over pilaf just before serving or serve in a separate bowl.

prawns in biz'har spices with spicy yellow rice

My earliest memories in the Gulf are of scooping up great handfuls of live Omani tiger prawns and cooking them up into a paella-style pilaf using the superb freshly roasted spices of my newly found *biz'har* spice mixture.

I adore taking off to the fish *souqs* of Dubai, or those on the East coast at Dibba or Fujeirah, or even meeting the fishing boats that come into the Jumeirah harbours along Dubai city's coast. The fish is fantastically fresh and the prices are good.

Prawns or shrimps are sold in categorised sizes, ranging from 8-50 per kilo. I like to use medium-sized Omani tiger prawns, or I select the 20-25 per kilo size, whichever is the freshest. Make sure they are all of the same size so that they cook evenly. **Serves 6-8 in the Middle East as a main course and 8-10 in the West.**

* 1.5 kg medium to large prawns
* 2 tablespoons *biz'har*, page 6
* 5 cups prawn or chicken stock
* 2 medium or 200g sliced red onions
* 4 crushed garlic cloves
* 5 medium or 400g finely chopped tomatoes
* 2 *loomi*
* a bunch of coriander, stalks only

* 5 cups or 1 kg basmati rice
* 2 tablespoons olive oil or more if necessary
* 1 teaspoon powdered *loomi*
* 2 sliced green chillies
* 1 teaspoon powdered turmeric
* 1 teaspoon crushed saffron strands
  soaked in 3 tablespoons boiling water
* sea salt and freshly ground black pepper

1 To prepare each prawn, pull the head from the prawn, peel off the shell and keep the tail on. Remove the black vein that runs along the back of the prawn; wash and set aside. Repeat with the remaining prawns. Sprinkle with *biz'har*, and set aside, while you crack on with the recipe.

2 To make the prawn stock, put the heads and shells in the water and add half the onions, half the garlic cloves, one of the tomatoes, both *loomi* and all the coriander stalks. Bring to the boil in a large saucepan; immediately reduce to a simmer for 15 minutes. Strain and reserve.

3 Meanwhile, prepare the rice, see page 25. Finally, cover with fresh water and leave to soak for about 10 minutes.

4 While the rice is soaking, heat half the olive oil in a large, heavy saucepan, and add the remaining sliced onions. Cook until they are well glazed, and caramelised, very crispy and golden brown, about 10 minutes on a medium to high heat. Add the remaining crushed garlic cloves and stir-fry for 1 minute. Add the prawns, powdered *loomi*, the green chilli and turmeric; season with 1 tablespoon of sea salt and freshly ground black pepper to taste. Stir-fry until the prawns are just pink, around 1 minute. Add the remaining tomatoes. Season with sea salt and freshly ground black pepper to taste and stir-fry for another 1-2 minutes.

5 Drain the rice and add to the saucepan; season with sea salt and freshly ground black pepper to taste. Stir-fry gently on a low heat to cover the rice grains with the flavours in the pan. Pour in 5 cups of prawn stock, as well as the saffron with its soaking water; stir once gently. Bring to the boil, uncovered, about 5-6 minutes; reduce the heat, re-cover, and simmer for 15 minutes or until the rice is cooked al dente. Uncover, stir twice to combine gently; cover and leave to stand for 5 minutes. To serve, turn out onto a serving dish or platter; pour over the butter or ghee and serve with fresh lime halves, cos leaves and my recipe for fresh tomato chutney, opposite.

Opposite: a traditional cooking pot for the
wedding feast of lamb and rice
Satwa, Dubai 1978

Below: the red sands of the Al Khatab Desert
United Arab Emirates 1977

FRESH TOMATO CHUTNEY
Mix together three skinned, seeded and
finely chopped tomatoes, one finely
chopped green pepper and one small
red onion. Squeeze over the juice of
two limes, season with sea salt and
freshly ground white pepper.
Leave to infuse for 10-15 minutes;
stir in a handful of coriander leaves
just before serving.

29

Mezze

crispy prawn, pine nut and feta sambousek rolls

Sambousek, oven-hot and tiny, are usually crescent-shaped or *samosa-style* triangular pies.

Traditional Gulf pastry is a type of short crust and requires practice and plenty of toil to make it melt in the mouth. For an easier option, I like rolling *sambousek* fillings in *filo* or spring roll wrappers to make rolls. I urge you to read the pastry packaging instructions well for tips on thawing, handling and baking before you begin. I chop all the ingredients individually in my blender, with a whizz on/off to chop, not purée them; then hand mix into a paste for the filling. **Makes around 27 rolls.**

filling:
2 teaspoons olive oil
4 tablespoons pine nuts
1/2 small or 80g roughly chopped onion
1 clove mashed garlic
1 small finely chopped red pepper
100g finely chopped prawns or shrimp
2/3 cup or 150g feta cheese
2 tablespoons chopped fresh mint leaves
sea salt and freshly ground white pepper
* 6 sheets *filo* pastry or 27 spring roll wrappers
* 2 heaped tablespoons melted butter or ghee
   egg wash:
   * 1 egg
   * 2 tablespoons water
   * a pinch of sea salt

hot chilli dip

* 1 teaspoon whole coriander seeds
* 1 teaspoon powdered cumin seeds
* 1 seeded and finely chopped red pepper
* 2 skinned, seeded and finely chopped tomatoes
* 2 teaspoons lime juice
* 1 teaspoon sugar
* 4 sliced red chillies
* 1 tablespoon extra virgin olive oil

1 Heat the oil in a small, non-stick pan and add the pine nuts. Stir-fry on a medium heat until golden brown, 30 seconds to 1 minute. Remove and set aside on a paper towel to drain. Place in a bowl.

2 Into the same pan, add the onion and stir-fry on a low heat until glazed and soft but without taking on any colour, about 2 minutes. Remove from the heat and add to the bowl. Add the garlic, red pepper, prawns or shrimp, feta and fresh mint leaves to the bowl. Stir well to combine. Season with freshly ground white pepper; feta is usually salty so you should not have to add additional salt. Weigh off the filling into tablespoonfuls, each weighing about 15 grams. Form into slender finger-shaped rolls about 5 centimetres long; place on a tray. Cover with cling wrap and leave in the fridge to firm.

3 Prepare the egg wash by beating all the ingredients together and set aside.

4 Thaw pastry out. Peel off one sheet; lay it down and brush it very, very lightly with a little melted butter or ghee. Place a second layer on top of the first and butter it carefully and lightly. With a knife, neatly cut the two layered sheets so that you have 9 rectangular strips (approximately 10 cm x 18 cm). To prevent pastry from drying out, cover with cling wrap whenever it is not in use.

5 Place the chilled filling at the short end of each strip. Fold the sides of the pastry over the filling; roll it up firmly. Brush the end with melted ghee to seal the roll. If the filling seems too big, simply remove some of it so that the pastry can wrap up and seal well. Repeat.

6 Preheat the oven to 190 °C.

7 Place rolls on a well-greased oven tray with the sealed end underneath; brush the top and sides with the egg wash. Bake in the preheated oven, about 25 minutes, or until golden and crispy. Serve immediately as an appetizer, as part of mezze or as a snack with the hot chilli dip, or with a prepared sauce such as *harissa*.

hot chilli dip

1 Place the coriander and powdered cumin seeds in a non-stick pan; dry-roast on a medium heat until their aroma perfumes the air, about 1 minute. Remove and place in a blender.

2 Place all the remaining ingredients, except the chillies, in the blender and whizz until blended. Remove and place in a bowl. Add the sliced red chillies and leave for at least 15 minutes to infuse before using. The chilli dip will last for up to three weeks in an airtight container if covered with an additional pour of olive oil to cover the surface of the dip completely.

Mezze is a brilliant way to start a party or barbecue. Crowd the centre of your table generously with these amazing Middle Eastern appetisers.
Their flavours and colours are astonishing as well as being scented with bright lemons, green skinned limes, herbs and sunny or grass-green olive oils.

I use pretty bowls and baskets filled with oven-warmed Arabic pitta breads, and flat plates piled high with whole sun-ripened and fresh scented red tomatoes, crisp fresh mint leaves, snappy lettuce hearts, glistening olives, and pickled green chillies.
Everyone helps themselves to the dishes and salads that take their fancy.

This page: fruit and vegetable souq
Shindaga, Bur Dubai 1978

All the recipes in this section
serve 4-6 as a starter
or 8-12 if served together
as mezze.

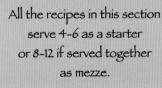

falafel kofta with tahina and tahina taratoor dip

This recipe is for a modern, fresh, finger-shaped light falafel with a golden crumb crust.
They are delicious on their own or dipped into fresh home-made, lemony, creamy
tahina taratoor; the combination can be wrapped in Arabic bread, *khoubz*, with sliced tomatoes, mint
leaves and shredded cos lettuce for a brilliant sandwich. Serve with various mezze such as *shankleesh*
(pictured below; recipe overleaf) with chillli, pickles and salads.

* 1/2 cup or 130g dried chickpeas
* 1 1/2 cups or 250g dried black-eyed peas
* 4 cloves mashed garlic
* 1 teaspoon powdered cumin seeds
* 1 cup loosely packed parsley leaves
* 1/2 cup loosely packed coriander leaves
* sea salt and freshly ground black pepper
* 2 roughly chopped red onions
* 1 teaspoon *tahina*
* 2 tablespoons lime juice
* 8 slices of toasted white bread
* olive oil for shallow frying

1 Soak the chickpeas and black-eyed peas together overnight in plenty of cool water, about 4 cups, as they will absorb roughly twice their volume; drain and place in a pan. Cover with plenty of fresh, cool water. Bring to the boil and reduce heat only a little because you need to maintain a steady boil for about 1 hour 15 minutes or until very tender. Ten minutes before the end of cooking, stir in one tablespoon of salt, or less if preferred; drain and place in a blender.

2 Place all the remaining ingredients, except the white bread and olive oil, in the blender. Season with sea salt and freshly ground black pepper to taste and whizz on/off a few times until just combined and roughly textured; do not over process to a purée. Taste and adjust the seasoning with additional sea salt or a little lime juice - not too much or the *falafel* mixture will not bind.

3 Divide the mixture into finger-shaped ovals weighing roughly 30 grams and place on a tray in the fridge for 30 minutes to firm up.

4 Leaving the crusts on, break the bread up and place in a blender. Whizz on/off until finely crumbed.

5 Remove the *falafel* from the fridge; roll them in the breadcrumbs to coat lightly. They may be kept in the fridge, placed on a tray and well covered with cling wrap, for up to 12 hours ahead of frying or they can be frozen at this stage. If frozen, allow to thaw in the fridge completely, and then continue with the next stage.

6 Heat a non-stick pan with a generous depth of olive oil to shallow fry the *falafel*.

7 Remove them from the fridge and fry until golden, turning to cook evenly; with a slotted spoon, remove and drain on a paper towel. Serve as appetisers, as part of mezze or as a filling in pitta breads. The recipe for tahina taratoor dip below is an ideal accompaniment.

tahina taratoor dip

* 1 cup *tahina*
* 1/2 cup lemon juice; 2-3 lemons
* 2 mashed garlic cloves
* 1 teaspoon sea salt
* 1/2 cup iced water

1 Blend all the ingredients together, except the water.

2 When blending, slowly pour in half a cup of the iced water until the mixture is creamy and has no resistance: the texture of a dipping sauce. You may well have to pour up to 1 cup of iced water to obtain a creamy texture.

3 Taste and adjust the seasoning with either a little more sea salt or a drop or two of lemon juice, taking care as too much will make it too liquid. Serve well chilled.

shankleesh

* 250g *labneh*
* 1-2 finely chopped red chillies
* juice of 2 limes
* 2 tablespoons extra virgin olive oil
* 1 tablespoon tomato sauce

Mix all the ingredients together until well combined.

closed for lunch, *gha'da*
Bur Dubai Souq 1977

fattoush with sumac vinaigrette

Amman, Jordan was where I first tucked into this outstanding Middle Eastern bread salad.
The essentials of sumac's uniquely lemony taste, which flavours the naturally sweet, sun-ripened
tomatoes, lives with me still. **Makes a large bowl for 6.**

* 1 thin Arabic bread
* 8-12 sliced cos lettuce leaves
* 2 chopped tomatoes
* sea salt and freshly ground pepper to taste
* 1 bunch *rocca* leaves, stalks removed
* 1/2 cup or 2 finely chopped spring onions
* 1/4 cup finely chopped flat leaf parsley
* 1/4 cup freshly chopped mint leaves
* 1 peeled and chopped cucumber
* 2-3 thinly sliced radishes, optional
* sea salt to taste and freshly ground black pepper
* a few fresh mint leaves and a sprinkling of sumac for garnish

sumac vinaigrette dressing:
4 tablespoons extra virgin olive oil
2 tablespoons lemon juice
juice of 1 lime
sea salt to taste and freshly ground black pepper
1/2 mashed clove garlic
2 tablespoons ground *sumac*
1 tablespoon boiling water

1 Preheat the oven to 160 °C.
2 Select the large, thin round flat Arabic breads. Cut into bite-sized pieces, spread on a baking tray and
toast until golden brown, about 8 minutes but watch carefully - they blacken easily.
3 Wash the lettuce and rocca leaves and place in a bowl of iced water. Leave for 10 minutes to crisp; then drain
and dry. Wrap loosely in cling wrap and place in the fridge. Repeat for watercress if using.
4 Place the tomatoes in a separate bowl and season with sea salt to taste, freshly ground black pepper and
a pinch of *sumac*. Leave for 15 minutes for the flavours to develop.
5 To serve, tear the salad leaves and place in a bowl. Add all the remaining salad ingredients, as well as the
tomatoes.
6 To make up the *sumac* salad dressing, mix all the ingredients together and shake well to combine. Pour over
the salad and toss gently to combine. Garnish with fresh mint leaves and shower with *sumac*; let
it stand for 5 minutes, and serve well chilled.

za'atar stuffed vine leaves

My vine leaf stuffing is first sautéed in extra virgin olive oil for plump, concentrated flavours bursting with the essence of the sunny Mediterranean. They can be made a day ahead; I pack them into an airtight container and cover with a light covering of extra virgin olive oil. Makes about 35-40 stuffed vine leaves.

* 1/2 cup Egyptian rice
* 4 tablespoons extra virgin olive oil
* 100g minced leg of lamb
* 1 teaspoon *za'atar* spice mixture
* 3 tablespoons pine nuts
* 1 finely chopped tomato
* 3 tablespoons powdered coriander seeds
* juice of 1 lemon
* 1 tablespoon finely chopped fresh mint leaves
* sea salt and freshly ground black pepper
    * 35-40 or a large jar of vine leaves
    * 2 cups chicken stock

                poaching stock:
                1 sliced onion
                1 sliced tomato
                1 star anise
                a few flat leaf parsley stalks with their leaves
                juice of 1 lemon

1 Soak the rice for 10 minutes and drain.

2 Heat 2 tablespoons of the extra virgin olive oil in a saucepan and add the minced lamb; season with sea salt, freshly ground black pepper and *za'atar*; stir-fry until golden brown and the perfume is released, about 2 minutes.

3 Add the pine nuts; stir-fry until golden brown and toasted. Quickly add the remaining ingredients, except for the vine leaves, and stir-fry for 2 minutes. Remove to a bowl and cool. No need to wash the saucepan.

4 Wash the vine leaves off gently to remove the brine solution in which they are preserved. Lay the leaves on a clean surface, vein side down. Place a tablespoonful, around 15 grams, of the mixture in the top, broad-end of the vine leaf. Fold the sides of the vine leaf over the filling and tightly roll up, similar to a spring roll.

5 Heat two tablespoons of the remaining extra virgin olive oil in the saucepan and add all the ingredients for the poaching stock. Stir-fry for 3 minutes on a low heat to loosen or deglaze the pan's seasonings. Remove from the heat; allow to cool, and pack the vine leaves tightly into the pan with the end leaf edge facing down.

6 Pour chicken stock over the vine leaves to cover; it may be necessary to add more stock, depending on the size of your pan. Cover with a plate to help weigh down the leaves to prevent them from floating. Simmer for about 30 minutes; remove the pan from the heat; leave the vine leaves to cool in the pan.

7 To serve, remove from the stock and place on a serving tray; drizzle over a thin pouring of extra virgin olive oil.

za'atar spice mixture

If dried *za'atar* is not available, substitute with a mixture of 1/4 cup dried thyme and 1/4 cup dried marjoram. It will keep in an airtight container if stored on a cool, dark shelf or in the fridge; use within 3 months.
Makes 1 cup.

* 3/4 cup sesame seeds   * 1/4 cup sumac
* 2 teaspoons sea salt   * 1/2 cup dried za'atar

1 Place the sesame seeds in a non-stick frying pan and dry-roast until golden. Remove and set aside.

2 Place the remaining ingredients in a grinder or small blender and grind until fine. Mix in the sesame seeds and whizz for a second or two. Store in an airtight container.

sumac

Sumac berries, *Rhus coriaria*, are tiny, red berry fruits, prized for their lemon flavour. Almost always used dried, either whole or ground, shower them over salads or use as a seasoning in stuffings and minced meat mixtures. Californian stoned, dried red cherries are an excellent substitute, either whole or finely chopped.

hommous with meat

An essential dip for mezze, its smooth and creamy, crushed sesame tahina and lemony flavours are marvellous when served with grilled or barbecued lamb kofta.

Dried chickpeas soaked overnight offer up more flavour then the tinned version; if you do use tinned chickpeas, drain and rinse them thoroughly in plenty of fresh running water before using. Try selecting tahina that is as white in colour as possible; the flavour seems to have a superior velvety-smooth quality. **Makes 2 cups.**

* 1 cup or 200g dried chickpeas
* 1/2 cup lemon juice from 2-3 lemons
* 1/4 cup ice-cold water
* 3 roughly chopped garlic cloves
* 1/4 teaspoon sea salt
* 1/4 cup plus 2 tablespoons tahina

meat garnish:
60g tiny diced leg of lamb
a pinch of freshly ground black pepper
a pinch of sea salt
2 tablespoons extra virgin olive oil
1-2 teaspoons powdered paprika for garnish

1 Soak the dried chickpeas overnight in plenty of fresh cool water as they will absorb three times their volume. Drain and bring to the boil in a large pot of water. Reduce the heat and simmer for 1 1/2 hours or until soft; drain.

2 Place the chickpeas in a blender with the lemon juice, garlic, salt and tahina. Whizz until well blended. With the machine on, slowly add the water and blend to a creamy paste. Taste for flavour and adjust by adding more sea salt or lemon juice if necessary; blend to mix well. Spoon the paste into a serving bowl and smooth it round to create a well in the centre.

3 For the lamb, rub the sea salt, freshly ground black pepper and 1 of the tablespoons of extra virgin olive oil into the lamb. Marinate for 10 minutes.

4 Decorate the hommous with the traditional paprika garnish: flatten paprika powder onto a plate; wet a fork and shake off any excess water; press the back of the wet fork into the paprika; knock off any excess paprika powder; press the fork gently onto the surface of the hommous; lift off and wash the fork. Repeat 5 or 6 times. Pour the diced lamb, with its marinade, into a hot non-stick pan and stir-fry until golden and cooked through. Spoon the meat into the well of the hommous and drizzle the remaining tablespoon of extra virgin olive oil over the meat. Serve with Arabic bread.

rocca salad with sumac

The sun-drenched, sandy farm plots of the Middle East raise bright green, crisp, mild and mustard-flavoured *rocca* leaves which, when showered with lemony rouge *sumac*, have unbeatable vibrancy.

Called variously *rocca*, rocket, *arugula* or *gir gir*, which is the Arabic, its soft dark leaves grow close to the sandy soil so they require careful, repeated washing and rinsing in plenty of fresh, cool water.

Choose an extra virgin olive oil with soft, grass-green hues that complement the bite and zest of the *rocca* perfectly. Alternatives to *rocca* are feathery leafed *mizuna* leaves with their mild mustard flavour.

* 4 bunches, or about 6 cups loosely packed *rocca* leaves
* 4 small, halved or quartered tomatoes
* 1 large, sliced red onion
* 1 teaspoon ground sumac powder for garnish

    lemony sumac salad dressing:

2 tablespoons apple vinegar	1 teaspoon ground sumac powder
1 teaspoon sugar	sea salt and freshly ground black pepper
4 tablespoons extra virgin olive oil	2 tablespoons boiling hot water

1 Wash the *rocca* leaves well until sand-free and clean; slice off the stalks. Fill a large bowl with ice cold water and add some ice cubes. Place the leaves in the water for 10 minutes to crisp. They bruise and crush very easily and need to be drained with gentle care; shake the excess water off gently or pat dry with a paper towel. Wrap loosely in cling wrap and place in the fridge to keep crisp.

2 Mix the lemony salad dressing ingredients together; set aside.

3 Just before serving, place the crisp *rocca* leaves in a large mixing bowl together with the onions and tomatoes. Pour over the dressing and toss gently. Transfer to a serving bowl and sprinkle the ground *sumac* powder over the top for garnish.

tabbouleh

The mint and flat-leafed parsley leaves release their radiant herby flavours,
vital, volatile and garden-green, to produce this finest of Middle Eastern
and Mediterranean salads.

This salad waits for no one; once chopped, serve immediately to taste fresh herby
flavours, which are otherwise quickly lost. Hand chopping is a necessary labour but, to
preserve the essence of the dish, a worthwhile slog. The amount of *burghul* and tomato
varies enormously, with a fair amount of national pride, from region to region throughout the
Middle East. However, I like crossing borders, using only a light dusting of *burghul* and plenty
of tomatoes. **Makes 4 cups.**

* 8 cups loosely packed flat parsley leaves
* 4 cups loosely packed mint leaves
* 3 tablespoons or 50g fine white *burghul*
* 3 skinned, seeded and finely chopped tomatoes
* 1-2 finely sliced spring onions

cumin salad dressing:
3 tablespoons lemon juice
2 teaspoons powdered cumin seeds
2 tablespoons extra virgin olive oil
1 tablespoon hot water
sea salt and white pepper

1 Wash the flat parsley and mint leaves and dry in a salad spinner or pat dry with a paper towel. Pick over
and select only the unblemished leaves, cover with cling wrap and leave to crisp in the fridge.
2 Pour the boiling water over the *burghul* and soak for 15 minutes to absorb the water and soften. Drain
and squeeze out any excess water.
3 To skin the tomatoes, see page 108. Chop the tomatoes and place in a large bowl with their juice; add lemon
juice, powdered cumin and extra virgin olive oil. Leave to soak to develop their flavours.
4 Meanwhile, finely chop the chilled parsley and mint leaves by hand. Place in the bowl with the tomatoes;
add the *burghul* mixture and the spring onions. Mix all the ingredients together gently, place in a serving bowl
and serve immediately.

Lentils

my lentil and lime soup

Closely resembling an old slow-cook recipe I was once given in Dubai in the seventies, the citrus notes cut through its earthy character to create a flavour of deep resonance and complexity.

Expect this to cook for a minimum of 2 hours, but don't begrudge the time. Steps one to three make up the stock, which can be made well in advance and frozen. If you cannot find *loomi*, just leave them out; this lentil soup is still worth making. For this recipe, I use whole brown lentils, *aka masoor*, or tiny red lentils, *masoor ke dal*, or yellow split peas, *toor ke dal*. **Serves 4-6.**

home-made stock:

1 kg chicken bones	6 roughly chopped garlic cloves
1 kg mutton or lamb bones	2 roughly chopped carrots
4 tablespoons olive oil	12 cups cold water
2 roughly chopped onions	2 bay leaves

* 380g or 2 cups brown lentils
* 1 teaspoon *biz'har*, page 6
1 teaspoon powdered coriander seeds
* 3 finely chopped tomatoes
* 2 tablespoons tomato purée
* 2 *loomi*
* juice of 3-4 limes
* juice of 2 lemons
* sea salt and freshly ground black pepper

1 To make the home-made stock, preheat oven to 190°C and roast the bones in a roasting tin with half the vegetables and 2 tablespoons olive oil; forget about them for 2-2 1/2 hours or until well browned. Transfer the bones to a large stock pan. Deglaze the pan juices in the roasting tin by adding a little water and stirring to loosen; add to the stock pan.

2 Add all the cold water and turn up the heat to full. Skim off any scum that immediately shows itself on the surface. Toss in one bay leaf.

3 Boil the stock; then immediately reduce the heat to a brisk simmer for 2-3 hours, skimming as necessary. Turn off the heat; let it cool and sieve the whole lot, reserving the stock and discarding the boiled bones and vegetables. Making the stock ahead to this stage is fine; it will keep refrigerated for up to 3 days and any solidified fat can be quite easily removed.

4 To make the soup, pour the last 2 tablespoons of olive oil into a large stock or soup pan. Add the remaining onions and garlic; stir-fry until well glazed and soft. Add the rest of the vegetables; season lightly with sea salt and freshly ground pepper; stir-fry the whole lot until you have vegetables of golden colour, which takes around 10 minutes.

5 Throw in the lentils, biz'har, the remaining bay leaf and coriander powder, stirring for 5 minutes on a low heat, until their roasted aromas scent the air. Add the tomatoes and the tomato purée; season lightly with a little sea salt and freshly ground pepper; stir-fry for another minute. Pour in the reserved chicken and lamb stock; add the loomi; bring to simmer, and simmer until the lentils are soft, about a further 10 minutes, adding more salt to taste.

6 Cool and blend. See caution, page 108. Pour in the lime juice and lemon juice; stir well and adjust the flavour for taste, adding more sea salt and freshly squeezed lime juice to taste. Serve with Arabic bread.

Middle Eastern lentil recipes are complex and deliciously unfathomable; their defining tastes are garnered from a stock made with both chicken and lamb bones, *loomi* and fresh limes, which contribute to making rich satisfying dishes of incomparable depth of flavour.

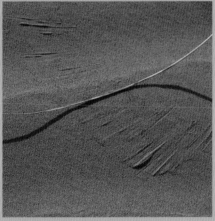

Perhaps more than any other, these lentil recipes are an amalgamation of all the characteristics that I most love in Middle Eastern food. Great aromas and rich colours are at the heart of cuisines hugely competent with the use of spices, producing enormously nourishing depths of meaty flavours, tart with lime juice and smooth with comfort.

loomi-scented dahl

Scented with *loomi*, this simple comfort food is perked up with the essential hot
garnish: the fragrance of curry leaves and the gusto of mustard seeds.
Although originally from the southern Indian cuisines, this Gulf version is less spicy; feel
free to omit the green chilli altogether if you prefer. Serve with fresh limes cut in half. I can
highly recommend pouring some of my ginger spiked *laban*, page 12, onto the rice and dahl for a
marvellous boost of tart flavour. **Serves 4-6 spooned over plain white basmati rice.**

* 2 tablespoons olive oil
* 1 finely chopped small onion
* 1 clove of mashed garlic
* 1/4 teaspoon turmeric powder
* 1 teaspoon powdered cumin seeds
* a pinch of cumin seeds
* 1 teaspoon *biz'har*, page 6
* 1 cup or 200g red lentils
* 1 sliced fresh green chilli

* 2 *loomi*
* 5 cups water
* 1 medium coarsely chopped tomato
* 1 teaspoon sea salt
* 2 bay leaves
* fresh coriander leaves for garnish

hot garnish:
2 tablespoons ghee or olive oil
2 cloves of mashed garlic
1 teaspoon mustard seeds
about 10 curry leaves

54

1 Heat the olive oil in a non-stick saucepan. Add the onion and stir-fry until glazed, transparent and golden. Add the garlic, turmeric powder, powdered cumin seeds, cumin seeds and *biz'har*; stir-fry until their fragrance fills the air and the cumin seeds begin to 'crackle' or splutter.

2 Add the red lentils, green chilli if using, and *loomi*; stir-fry for a couple of minutes. Pour in the water; add the tomatoes and bay leaves; season with sea salt and simmer for a further 20-22 minutes or until the lentils are cooked al dente and the water is thickened.

3 Just before serving, prepare the hot garnish by heating the *ghee* or olive oil in a separate non-stick pan. Add the garlic; stir-fry for a couple of minutes. Add the mustard seeds and curry leaves; stir-fry until the mustard seeds 'crackle' or splutter. Pour into the *dahl* and stir thoroughly. Serve in a bowl, shower with fresh coriander leaves, and spoon over cooked basmati rice.

basmati rice

I like to lavish care on the fine nutty aromas and flavours in basmati rice grains, which are lengthened by a careful cooking process, becoming fluffy and separate. **Serves 3 in the Gulf and Asia as the main dish and 4-5 in the West as an accompaniment to a main dish.**

* 2 cups basmati rice   * 1 teaspoon sea salt
* 2 cups fresh water   * 1 teaspoon olive oil

1 Wash and rinse the rice, see HANDLING, page 25. Place in a medium-sized, 20 centimetre diameter saucepan with 2 cups of fresh, salted water. Stir in the olive oil. Ensure that the level of the water is 1 centimetre above the level of the rice.

2 Cover with a tightly fitting lid; turn on the heat, simmer for 12 minutes and turn off the heat. Leave to stand, without removing the lid, for another 5 minutes. Check that all the water has been absorbed and the rice fluffs up easily with a fork; leave to stand a little longer if necessary.

The best way to cook the
basmati rice is to use the
absorption method, but it does
mean trying out the correct size
of saucepan, which is critical to
the success of this method.
The water should cover the rice
by 1 centimetre only.

Jumeirah coastal sunset
Dubai 1977

If it is too deep or too shallow,
change your pan accordingly.
Once you have mastered the
size of the pan, cooking perfect
fluffy rice every time is easy.
Dahl is always served over
cooked white rice.

Fish

barbecued red snapper

Crispy barbecued red snapper skin is a feast all on its own and its fine white, sweet meat is a treasure. The flames for a barbecue fire will take at least 30 minutes to burn down to reveal red-hot coals covered in a fine white ash; this is the optimum point at which to start to barbecue. I choose a non-stick grid which simplifies the job of barbecuing the delicate red snapper, *sammach hamrah mishwee*. **Serves 6**; this dish goes particularly well with white rice or vermicelli rice, a bowl of freshly cut limes and rocca salad.

* 1 x 3.5 kg or 2 x 1.5 kg red snapper or similar white fish; scaled and gutted
* sea salt and freshly ground white pepper

>*biz'har loomi marinade:*
>3 mashed garlic cloves
>3 cardamom pods
>4 cm cinnamon bark
>1/2 teaspoon turmeric
>1 teaspoon paprika powder
>1/2 cup lemon juice, 2-3 lemons
>1 *loomi*, seeds removed
>1 tablespoon olive oil

1 Season the fish with sea salt and freshly ground white pepper and place in a large pan. Mix and grind all the ingredients of the *biz'har loomi* marinade together; pour inside and over the fish to coat well. Cover with cling wrap and marinate for 20 minutes.

2 When the barbecue is ready, place the fish on the grid and cook for 15 minutes; turn it over and cook for another 10 minutes if you like fish just cooked, and for 15 minutes if you like fish well done. Test and cook longer if necessary; serve quickly.

vermicelli rice

Serves 8-10 in the Gulf and Asia and 10-12 in the West.

* 1 kg or 5 cups basmati rice
* 3 tablespoons olive oil
* 2 tablespoons *ghee* or butter
* 1 1/2 cups or 120g vermicelli
* 3 bruised and split cardamom pods
* 2 tablespoons sea salt
* 7 cups cold water

1 Prepare the rice, see HANDLING, page 25. Cover with fresh, cold water and leave to soak for about 15 minutes; drain and set aside.

2 Heat the olive oil and ghee or butter in a large thick-bottomed saucepan or cast-iron casserole. Add the vermicelli and cardamom and stir-fry until the cardamom perfumes the air and the vermicelli takes on a light golden colour, about three minutes. Add the drained rice and sea salt; stir-fry for about 3 minutes to coat the rice grains with the flavours in the pan.

3 Pour in the cold water and bring to the boil uncovered; immediately reduce the heat to a simmer; cover and cook for 15 minutes; at this stage all the water should have been absorbed by the rice. Turn off the heat and leave covered for a further 5 minutes, allowing the rice to stand and steam in the saucepan. Pile onto a platter or serving bowl. Please note that the cardamom pods are not meant to be eaten so you may prefer to remove them before serving.

Heading down in the early morning
to the shoreline or corniche fish
markets, *souqs*, in this region is a
treat; a favourite pastime of mine
is to savour the crush and clamour
of haggling buyers viewing the
piles of fish, *sammach*, brought
straight from the boats.

Palm frond fishing boat
Fujairah 1977

Enormous varieties of fish, each
in abundance, are astonishingly
fresh: bright-eyed, shiny, slippery,
wriggling and glistening. *Souq*
buying is a unique experience
where you will find some of the
finest fish you are ever
likely to see.

fennel smoked biz'har roast hammour with spicy tomato sauce and couscous

Full of deep marine robust flavour, *hammour* is a massively meaty, firm-grained, sweet white fish of the grouper family; it is, and rightly so, enormously popular in the Gulf.

Dates and fish together are no strangers in Gulf cuisine, and strike a deep resonance; traditionally they are always served as accompaniments for fish and rice pilaf, *machboos sammach*.

I like to roast the fennel seeds first in a smoking hot pan and then add them to a *biz'har* and date syrup, *dibbs*, marinade. Its smoky fennel flavour of anise marries particularly well with the fine flavours of *hammour*. If you cannot get hold of *dibbs*, substitute with dark honey.

Any firm white fish such as trevally, *halwayoo*, monkfish, turbot or cod works well as a substitute for *hammour*. I serve it with either rice or couscous and my spicy tomato sauce recipe, page 90, cooked down to a deep red, pebbled with chopped green pepper and a handful of black olives, spritzed with lime, and showered with fresh coriander leaves. **Serves 6.**

* 6 x 180-200g hammour fillet
* 2 tablespoons plain or all-purpose flour
* 3-4 tablespoons olive oil for pan roasting
* fresh coriander sprigs for garnish

biz'har, dibbs and smoky fennel marinade:

1 teaspoon *biz'har*, page 6
1 clove mashed garlic
1 tablespoon *dibbs*
3/4 cup lemon juice; 3-4 lemons
1/2 teaspoon sea salt and finely ground black pepper
2 teaspoons olive oil
1 teaspoon fennel seeds

1 To make the marinade, blend together all the ingredients, except the fennel and olive oil. Pour the olive oil into a small non-stick, thick-bottomed frying pan and, when hot, add the fennel seeds and stir-fry rapidly for 30 seconds to 1 minute only. They will splutter and dance in the smoking hot oil. Carefully pour the fennel seeds and olive oil into the marinade mixture; blend until smooth.

2 Place the fish fillets in a bowl. Pour the marinade over to coat well; cover with cling wrap and leave in the fridge for up to 30 minutes.

3 Prepare the couscous and summery tomato sauce recipes. Both may be made in advance.

4 Heat the oil to medium hot for pan roasting the fish in a thick-bottomed, non-stick frying pan. Remove fish from the marinade and lightly dust both sides with flour by shaking the flour through a sieve over the fish to coat evenly; season lightly with salt and pepper. Place the fish in the pan and let it bubble for 3 minutes on one side, scooping the pan juices over the fish. Flip the fish fillets gently over to cook on the other side, also scooping the pan juices over the fish, for about 5-6 minutes or until just cooked through. Add the marinade and let it bubble for 3 minutes until the fish is well glazed. Serve immediately with couscous and summery tomato sauce and garnish with a sprig of coriander.

couscous and summery tomato sauce

Serves 6.

* 3 cups medium grained couscous
* 3 cups chicken stock
* 1 teaspoon sea salt
* spicy tomato sauce, page 90

* 1 green pepper, all white pith removed and cut into medium-sized dice
* about 20 black olives
* juice of 2-3 limes
* 2 teaspoons chopped fresh coriander leaves

1 Measure out the couscous into a large ovenproof bowl. Pour over the stock and add the salt. Stir gently with a slotted spoon until the stock has been absorbed evenly by the couscous. Cover with cling wrap and let it stand. To reheat and fluff up, place it in the microwave for 5-6 minutes or steam in a preheated oven (190°C) for 15 minutes or until hot.

2 Make up the spicy tomato sauce recipe and, when just bubbling, add the green pepper, black olives, lime juice and coriander leaves. Simmer for 5 minutes and serve with the couscous and fish.

BUYING The eyes should be firm and bright, not soft, flat or sunken. Check the skin and scales; they should be firm and shiny with good glistening colour. The gills should demonstrate freshly caught, bright pinkish-red vigour; dark red and dull with a fishy smell indicates that the fish is well past its sell by date.

PREPARATION Ask the fishmonger to prepare the fish just right for the recipe: gutted, trimmed, boned, scaled and either kept whole, or butterflied, or filleted, or cut into steaks.

TO TEST IF DONE The fish will flake when pierced with a toothpick.

crispy red mullet

Called *Sultan Ibrahim*, red mullet is one of the Middle East's darling fish, with fine white fillets, sweet and juicy, and gorgeous crispy red skin.

I like serving them with homemade French fries, the soft crunch of sea salt, the recipe for taratoor tahina dip, page 36 and plenty of fresh-cut lemons and limes. **Serves 4-5 as a main course with rice and salads.**

* 1.2 kg gutted red mullet, each around 100 grams
* salt and freshly ground black pepper
* 2 tablespoons flour
* olive oil for shallow frying

biz'har saffron marinade:
2 pinches of saffron, ground to a powder
a pinch of powdered cardamom
a pinch of powdered clove
 teaspoon powdered cinnamon
 teaspoon powdered turmeric
 teaspoon powdered paprika
juice of 1 lime
juice of 1 lemon
1 mashed garlic clove

1 Gently rub the inside and the skin of the fish with sea salt and freshly ground pepper; place in a large bowl. Mix the *biz'har* saffron marinade, pour over the fish and rub in gently. Cover with cling wrap and marinate for 5-10 minutes in the fridge.

2 Remove fish carefully from the marinade and set aside. Dust with flour to cover.

3 Heat the olive oil to medium hot. Gently slip the fish into the oil with a fish slice. Caution: there will be some splutter. Fry for 3 minutes on one side until crisp; turn them over gently and fry for an additional 2 minutes; test if done and fry for another minute if necessary. Remove; they do tend to break easily, so great care needs to be taken when lifting them out of the oil; place on a serving plate and serve immediately with the suggested accompaniments.

Egyptian rice stuffed roast chicken

Marinated in *biz'har* spices, this roasted chicken is tasty with
its magnificent stuffing of fat, soft rice grains and apricots, dates and lemony *sumac*.
Try serving it with the vermicelli rice page 60, a side dish of stuffed marrow page 22, and plates of
salad leaves, garlic chives, and freshly cut limes. **Serves 6.**

* 1 x 1.3-1.4 kg washed and dried chicken
* sea salt and freshly ground black pepper

> *biz'har roast marinade:*
> 4 tablespoons olive oil
> 1 teaspoon *biz'har*, page 6
> 1 teaspoon cumin seeds
> 2 cardamom pods
> 1 teaspoon fennel seeds
> 1 teaspoon coriander seeds

stuffing:
1/2 cup or 100g Egyptian rice
1 cup boiling water or home-made stock, page 50-52
2 whole wheat *pitta* breads or 3 slices brown bread
a handful, about 1/4 cup chopped coriander leaves
a handful, about 1/4 cup chopped parsley leaves
1 small roughly chopped onion
1 mashed garlic clove
4 apricots
5 or 50g stoned dates
1/2 cup or 70g sultanas
4 tablespoons or 40g pine nuts
1 teaspoon extra virgin olive oil
1 teaspoon *sumac*

1 Place the chicken in a large bowl. Blend all the marinade ingredients in a small blender or grinder until the spices are finely ground. Smear over the skin and the inside of the chicken; season with sea salt and pepper; cover with cling wrap and leave in the fridge to marinate for 30 minutes.

2 To make the stuffing, measure out the rice into a large mixing bowl and pour over two-thirds or 200 ml of the boiling water or chicken stock. Let it soak for 15 minutes. Toast the bread; break up roughly and place in a blender. Whizz on/off until roughly chopped. Add the handfuls of coriander and parsley leaves and whizz on/off until the mixture resembles breadcrumbs; scrape out and put in the mixing bowl with the rice and soaking liquid. Do not wash the blender; add the onion, garlic, apricots and dates and whizz on/off until finely chopped; remove and add to the mixing bowl. Add the sultanas.

3 Place the pine nuts in a non-stick, thick-bottomed pan with the extra virgin olive oil and stir-fry on a low heat until roasted golden, about 2 minutes. Remove and add to the mixing bowl; add the *sumac*, season well with sea salt and freshly ground black pepper and mix well to combine all the ingredients.

4 Preheat the oven to 200 °C.

5 I like to stuff the chicken to capacity; as it cooks, the stuffing will swell and spill into the pan, becoming roasted and well browned, deliciously texturising the soft stuffing. Line a roasting pan with foil and place a roasting rack over it; lightly oil the foil and rack. Place the stuffed chicken onto the rack; season by smearing any of the marinade juices over the chicken and, if you feel it necessary, season again with a light sprinkling of sea salt and freshly ground pepper.

6 Place in the preheated oven and roast for 30 minutes. Pull out of the oven; baste the pan juices over the chicken. Tear off and oil a piece of foil to cover the stuffing; leave the chicken uncovered and replace in the oven. Roast for another 45 minutes. Remove from the oven; check that the juices from the thigh run clear when pierced with a skewer; if pink, replace in the oven and roast until the juices run clear. Place the chicken on a serving plate; scoop up all the stuffing to serve with it and carefully remove the foil. Rest it for 15 minutes, keeping it warm, and then serve with the suggested accompaniments.

I was given a variation of this recipe for stuffed roast chicken by a Bahraini, who told me, 'use your imagination and stuff it with whatever fruits you like.' So I did; the dates and ground lemony *sumac* berries are mine. Feel free to add whichever dried fruits you want: blueberries, raspberries, or dried, red Californian cherries.

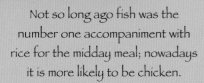

dhows on Dubai Creek 1977

Not so long ago fish was the number one accompaniment with rice for the midday meal; nowadays it is more likely to be chicken.

Try to buy organically reared chicken or at least corn-fed, free-range chickens; the meat will be leaner, tastier, and have a superior grained texture.
They are generally bigger, too, which means more meat.
Their carcasses are valuable and should not be discarded; use for making stock for soups or stews, pages 50-52.

chicken saloona

At most lunchtimes, lemon-fragranced *loomi* perfumes traditional chicken or fish and vegetable one-pot stews in an aromatic reduction of rich red sun-ripened tomatoes and coriander. Delicious served with a platter of white rice or vermicelli rice pilaf, salads such as white radish, cos lettuce, fresh-cut limes, and garlic chives, coriander leaves or watercress. I love to scatter my *saloona* with both freshly chopped dill and coriander. **Serves 6-8.**

vegetables:

* * 2 peeled potatoes
* * 4 baby marrow or 1 zucchini
* * 1 green bell pepper, trimmed of its white pith
* * 2 cups or 300g peeled butternut pumpkin
* * 3 small oval eggplants
* 6 ripe, red tomatoes
* 1 cup loosely packed, fresh coriander leaves
* 3 tablespoons cooking oil
* 1 x 1.5 kg chicken, skinned and jointed into 8-12 pieces
* 2 medium finely chopped onions
* 5 crushed garlic cloves
* 2 teaspoons grated fresh ginger
* 3 tablespoons tomato paste
* 3 small chopped green chillies
* 3 cups water or chicken stock
* 3 *loomi*
* freshly chopped dill and coriander for garnish, optional

loomi scented saloona biz'har:

2 teaspoons seeded powdered *loomi*

1 teaspoon turmeric powder

3 teaspoons coriander seeds

1 teaspoon powdered coriander seeds

1 teaspoon cloves

5g or 2 cinnamon sticks

1 teaspoon powdered cumin seeds

1/2 teaspoon powdered black pepper

3 lightly bruised cardamom pods

1 Prepare all the vegetables and measure out the *biz'har* spices; bash those whole spices that need pulverising in a pestle and mortar; reserve and set aside.

2 Place the tomatoes and fresh coriander leaves in a blender. Whizz on/off to chop finely and set aside.

3 Heat the olive oil in a large thick-bottomed pan, add the chicken pieces; lightly season with sea salt and freshly ground black pepper and stir-fry until golden brown, about 10 minutes; remove and set aside. To the same pan, add all the chopped vegetables, season with sea salt and pepper and stir-fry for about 12 minutes. When tinged with golden colour, remove and set aside.

4 Add the onions and stir-fry until well glazed and golden brown. Stir in the garlic, ginger, tomato paste, green chillies and the *biz'har*; stir-fry together for 1 minute. Add the tomatoes and coriander. Lightly season and stir well to combine.

5 Replace the chicken pieces into the saucepan over the tomatoes - no need to stir. Pour in the water or chicken stock, add *loomi* and bring to a simmer, uncovered, about 7 minutes. Cover and simmer on a low heat for 30 minutes or until the chicken is just tender.

6 Add the reserved vegetables; stir in gently and simmer for 10 minutes or until cooked al dente and the chicken is tender. Serve hot with the suggested accompaniments. **Note** that the whole spices are not meant to be eaten.

Arabic stews seem like a marathon preparation. However, this spectacular chicken stew, *saloona*, cooks itself, poaching in its own plentiful juicy stock, crammed with vegetables and all things coriander, brimming with rich red tomato flavour.

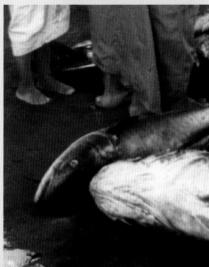

Opposite: Salalah fish souq
Oman, circa 1960s
picture by Hale Allen

During the holy month of *Ramadan*, *saloona* becomes a thick-gravied stew called *fareed* with the addition of thin Arabic bread, *raggag*, lining the bottom of the dish. Serve with cooked rice, at least one stuffed vegetable dish, *kousa meshwee*, soups, *sambousek*, dates, date desserts, *umm ali*, drinking yogurt or *laban*, sweetmeats, chocolates, tea and coffee.

spicy biz'har-basted barbecued quails

Marinated overnight in a fennel bath of mildly spicy flavours, tiny quail are delicious basted and then barbecued over a fire. The quails are first basted to tender perfection in their marinade juices, then flash barbecued for smoky flavour. Serves 4-8 as a side dish in the Middle East and 4 as a main course in the West. It also makes an excellent starter for 8.

* 8 oven-ready spatchcock quails
* 3 cloves garlic
* 4-5 tablespoons olive oil for pan roasting
* 1 cup water or chicken stock
* sea salt and finely ground black pepper

biz'har, dibbs and fennel marinade:
1 teaspoon mild *biz'har*, page 6
1 teaspoon fennel seeds
1 tablepoon *dibbs*
3/4 cup lemon juice; 3-4 lemons
1 teaspoon medium strength Indian masala powder

1 Place the prepared quails in a bowl, ensuring that they are clean with innards removed.

2 Blend together until smooth 2 tablespoons of the olive oil and all the ingredients for the marinade. Smear over the quails to coat well; cover the bowl with cling wrap and leave in the fridge overnight. If the quails started as frozen, they should thaw completely in the fridge during the marinating process.

3 Heat the remaining olive oil to a medium heat in a thick-bottomed, non-stick pan. Place the quails and the garlic in the pan; pour in the marinade juices together with the chicken stock or water. Leave to simmer, breast side up, partially covered, for 15 minutes. Meanwhile, prepare the barbecue; make sure that the flames have burnt off and that the coals are red hot and covered with a white ash.

4 When the fire is ready, place the quails on a well-oiled grid and barbecue on both sides, basting frequently, until they are tender and cooked through, about 15 minutes. Serve immediately.

freekeh risotto with green herbs and broad beans

Freekeh, or creamy soft young, roasted green wheat, is cooked risotto-style, spiked with cinnamon bark and budded with young green broad beans. In the Middle East *freekeh* is usually cooked in a stock, and then served as a glossy pilaf showered with meat, raisins, pistachios, almonds and pine nuts. I like to cook it like risotto, making it really lustrous, moist and creamy, pure velvety bliss. *Freekeh*, which is a naturally green colour, lends itself to a marriage with greens such as chopped dill and chopped coriander as well as the crunch of crushed pistachios. Serves 4 as a main meal and around 6–8 as an accompaniment to barbecued or roasted main course, such as Barbecued Quail.

* 2 cups or 300g *freekeh*
* 5 cups water
* 1 teaspoon sea salt
* 1 tablespoon olive oil
* 200g young frozen broad beans
* 3 tablespoons butter
* 1 teaspoon or large pinch of saffron strands
  soaked in 3 tablespoons of boiling water

* 1 medium finely chopped onion
* 1 mashed garlic clove
* 1 cup chicken stock or lamb stock
* 1/2 cup chopped dill
* 1/4 cup chopped coriander
* 1/4 cup roasted crushed pistachios for garnish

1 To parboil the *freekeh*, place in a bowl and rinse under running water, as for rice HANDLING, page 25. Fill a large saucepan with fresh, salted water and olive oil. Add the rinsed *freekeh* and bring to the boil, uncovered, stirring occasionally for about 6 minutes. Cover the saucepan with a tightly fitting lid. Reduce the heat and simmer for 15 minutes. Drain and set aside. Cover with cling wrap or refrigerate until needed.

2 Bring a second saucepan of water to the boil and add the frozen broad beans. Simmer for 5 minutes; drain and, when cool, peel and place in a bowl. The beans slip out of their skins easily when pressed gently between forefinger and thumb. Cover the bowl with cling wrap and refrigerate until needed.

3 Melt the butter in a non-stick, heavy saucepan. Add the onions and garlic; stir-fry on a medium to low heat for 4-5 minutes until the onions become glazed without taking on too much colour. Add the *freekeh* to the pan and stir gently to coat with the pan flavours. Season lightly with sea salt and freshly ground black pepper. Add one-third of the stock and stir gently until all the stock has been absorbed into the *freekeh*.

5 Repeat with the remaining two-thirds stirring until all the stock has been absorbed; if the *freekeh* seems a little dry or undercooked, add a little more stock and cook for a little longer. Just before serving, throw in all the herbs, the saffron with its water and the reserved peeled broad beans. Ensure that the *freekeh* grains are cooked al dente before serving. Taste and adjust the seasoning, shower with the pistachios, then serve immediately.

Barbecued quail is a centuries-old speciality of the Middle East and I serve mine with my modern recipe for *freekeh* risotto with green herbs, broad beans and the nutty rocca salad.

Quails are enjoying a revival. Most supermarkets stock oven-ready quails in frozen packs of eight, if fresh ones are unavailable. You can ask the butcher to spatchcock them, but it just means cutting out the backbone with a pair of scissors to flatten open like a book.

hazel nut and almond rocca salad

Make up the recipe for *rocca* salad with *sumac*, page 47, adding a teaspoon of honey to the dressing. Heat half a teaspoon of extra virgin olive oil in a non-stick pan and stir-fry a quarter cup of roughly crushed hazel nuts and a quarter cup of slivered almonds until golden. Remove and toss gently into the dressed *rocca* salad and serve immediately.

Lamb

lamb and okra stew

Suffused in a rich, freshly made tomato sauce reduction, fragrant with fresh coriander and spices, juicy leg of lamb chunks nestle in tender okra.

A firm favourite, okra is part of an extraordinarily delicious hot garnish with garlic, ginger and coriander. Syrians choose tiny okra, and only a slightly larger size of okra goes into Saudi lamb and okra stew recipes; either may be used for this Middle Eastern favourite.

The finger-long variety, called 'ladies' fingers', is never used. Frozen okra works excellently and I routinely use it for this recipe. I like the meat to be cut into large chunks; the juices are lost if cut smaller. **Serves 6-8 in the Middle East as an accompaniment to a large platter of rice or pilaf and serves 6 as a main course in the West.**

* 900g leg of lamb, cut into large chunks
* 4 crushed garlic cloves
* 4 tablespoons olive oil
* 3 medium chopped onions
* 2 tablespoons roughly broken coriander seeds
* 2 teaspoons *biz'har*, page 6
* 2 teaspoons cumin seeds
* 5 bruised and split cardamom pods
* 3 cloves
* 2 sliced green chillies

* 1 *loomi*
* 1 kg skinned, seeded and finely chopped tomatoes
* sea salt and freshly ground black pepper
* 3 cups water or lamb stock
* 1 tablespoon butter, *ghee* or olive oil
* 250g frozen okra
* 1 teaspoon peeled and grated fresh ginger root
* 1/4 cup freshly chopped coriander

1 Pour one tablespoon of olive oil and half the garlic into a bowl with the meat chunks. Season lightly with sea salt and pepper. Rub the garlic, salt, pepper and oil into the meat to coat well. Marinate at room temperature, covered, for 15 minutes or longer.

2 Heat one tablespoon of the remaining olive oil in a large, heavy saucepan; add the meat in batches and stir-fry on a medium to high heat to brown well and seal in the juices; remove to a bowl and set aside. Heat 1 tablespoon of oil; quickly add the onions and stir-fry until soft, transparent and well browned, about 5 minutes.

3 Bash the coriander in a pestle and mortar until roughly broken; add to the pan along with the *biz'har*, cumin, cardamom pods and cloves. Stir-fry on a medium heat until the spices perfume the air, around 2 minutes; be careful not to burn the spices and fragments on the bottom of the saucepan. Add a little water if the pan seems too hot. Add the green chilli, *loomi* and tomatoes; season lightly with sea salt and freshly ground black pepper.

4 Add the water or stock and bring to the boil; reduce the heat to simmer, uncovered, for half an hour or until the tomato sauce is reduced by two-thirds, about 4 cups, and beginning to thicken. Replace the meat; stir in, and simmer on a low heat, covered, for 20-25 minutes or until tender.

5 Fifteen minutes before serving, heat the last tablespoon of olive oil in a separate non-stick pan and add the ginger, remaining garlic and freshly chopped coriander; stir-fry for 30 seconds and then add the frozen okra. Season lightly with sea salt and freshly ground black pepper; stir-fry quicky for 2 minutes. Add to the lamb stew and simmer, uncovered, for about 2 minutes. Shower with chopped coriander.

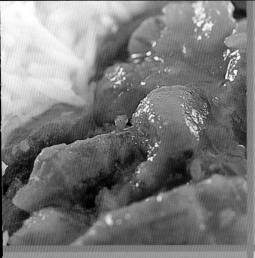

Poached lamb in spicy *biz'har* produces succulent stews called *saloona,* in Arabic. The stews are crammed with vegetables and their velvety soft meat glistens in scrumptious sauces. Lamb or goat, called Indian mutton, is cooked mostly on the bone for flavour.

For best results try to make your own stock, page 50, so that the end flavour is doubly enriched, doubly satisfying. The recipes for basmati rice, page 56, or the vermicelli rice, page 60, are good choices as accompaniments.

white bean stew

Aromatically infused soft white beans naturally thicken this exquisite recipe for a slow cooked, juicy, tender lamb stew.

Deep, wonderfully juicy flavours and aromas fill the house - aromas that come only from slow cooking and tender loving care. Just before serving, the hot garnish perfumes the dish superbly. Do not be put off by slow cooking; the preparation time is just 15 minutes and the cooking time will take 1 hour and 15 minutes leaving you free to do something else. I like sliced small neck fillets of lamb on the bone; if they are unavailable, use a half and half mixture of stewing lamb and small lamb loin chops. Serves 10-12 in the Middle East and serves 10 as a main course meal in the West. Hot *pitta* breads, the basmati rice recipe, page 56, or couscous are good choices as accompaniments.

* 1 1/2 cups or 225g dried white beans
* 1.5 kg lamb cubes on the bone, see notes above
* 1 tablespoon mild *biz'har*, page 6
* 1 tablespoon roughly broken cumin seeds
* sea salt to taste and freshly ground black pepper
* 3 tablespoons olive oil
* 5 cups or 1.25 litres water

* 2 medium chopped red onions
* 5 mashed garlic cloves
* 5 large or 1kg tomatoes, peeled seeded and diced
* 3 cups water or stock, pages 50-52
* 2 bay leaves
* 2 *loomi* broken or cut in half
* 6g or about 8 fresh *za'atar* or thyme leaves

warm garnish:
2 cloves mashed garlic
1 tablespoon butter or olive oil
4 tablespoons chopped fresh coriander

1 Soak the beans in 5 cups water overnight or for at least 12 hours.

2 Place the meat in a mixing bowl. Rub the *biz'har*, cumin, sea salt, freshly ground black pepper and 1 tablespoon of the olive oil into the meat and leave to marinate, covered, in the fridge, also for at least 12 hours.

3 Drain the beans; bring to the boil in 5 cups of water. Boil briskly, partially covered, for 1 hour; set aside.

4 Meanwhile, begin to cook the meat stew by heating a tablespoon of the olive oil in a large, heavy saucepan or casserole. Add the meat to the pan in batches and stir-fry on a high heat until well-browned, careful not to burn the spices on the bottom of the saucepan and adding a tablespoon or two of water to the pan if it seems too hot. Remove to a bowl and set aside. Quickly add the onions to the saucepan and stir-fry until soft, transparent and well browned. Add the garlic; stir-fry for a minute, then add the bay leaves, *loomi*, *za'atar* or thyme sprigs, and tomatoes; season with salt and pepper and stir-fry together for a couple of minutes. Return the meat to the pan.

5 Pour in the stock and bring to the boil; immediately reduce to a very low heat and gently simmer, partially covered, for 1 hour. Stir in the beans and their cooking water. Simmer for 15 minutes. If serving later, leave to cool, covered; when needed, reheat by simmering for 30 minutes.

6 To make the warm garnish, heat the olive oil in a frying pan on a medium heat. Add the garlic, remaining *za'atar* or thyme and coriander; stir-fry for 1 minute and stir into the stew. Serve immediately.

lamb kofta in spicy tomato sauce

Firing up a barbecue in the evening under a desert sky is a sensory treat; the laughter of children playing, the soft evening breeze over the cooling desert sands and the rich aromas from many other barbecues fill the air.

Grilled or barbecued kofta are a mouth-watering and quintessentially Middle Eastern evening meal.
I often oven grill them and serve, juicy and tender, over my recipe for freshly made spicy tomato sauce.
Serves 6 with Arabic bread, pickles, salads and a selection of *mezze*, particularly *hommous*.

sumac flavoured lamb kofta

* 500g freshly minced leg of lamb
* 2 medium quartered onions
* 1/4 cup coriander
* 1/4 cup parsley
* 1/4 cup mint
* 1 tablespoon mild *biz'har*, page 6
* 2 tablespoons *sumac*
* 1 tablespoon sea salt and freshly ground black pepper

1 Place the minced lamb in a mixing bowl.

2 Place all the remaining ingredients into the blender and whizz on/off until the onions and herbs are finely chopped. Scrape out into the mixing bowl with the lamb; hand mix, using wet, clean hands to combine well.

3 Shape into 8 x 70g rolls and thread onto skewers. Cover in cling wrap and set aside in the fridge for about an hour to firm up.

4 Prepare the fire and when the flames have burnt off and the coals are red-hot and covered with white ash, brush the kofta with olive oil, place on a well-oiled grid and barbecue for about 8 minutes, turning them with tongs so that they brown evenly. As they dry out quickly, serve immediately with the spicy tomato sauce, see overleaf.

spicy tomato sauce

* 1/4 cup fresh coriander leaves
* 2 medium peeled and quartered onions
* 2 tablespoons olive oil
* 1 teaspoon whole coriander seeds
* 1 teaspoon powdered coriander seeds
* 6 quartered large ripe tomatoes, stalk ends removed and seeds discarded
* 2 finely sliced green chillies
* 3 cloves mashed garlic
* 1 teaspoon dried oregano
* 1 1/2 teaspoons sea salt and freshly ground black pepper
* 1 cup water

1 Put the coriander leaves in a small blender and whizz on/off until finely chopped. Place in a bowl and reserve. Do not wash out the blender; finely chop the onions.
2 Heat the olive oil in a medium saucepan. When the oil is hot, add the chopped onions and cook for 5-8 minutes until soft and transparent; stir from time to time so that they cook evenly without taking on too much colour. Bash the coriander seeds in a pestle and mortar until roughly crushed and add to the pan. Add the coriander powder and stir-fry for 1 minute. Quickly add the finely chopped tomatoes, chilli, garlic and dried oregano. Season with sea salt and freshly ground black pepper and stir-fry for 3 minutes.
3 Stir in the water. Bring the sauce to a simmer and cook, uncovered, until the sauce thickens, about 10 minutes. Set aside and keep warm. The sauce can be made in advance and freezes well. When needed, thaw and reheat over a gentle heat until properly cooked through. Just before serving, add the reserved chopped coriander.

Above: broad beans or *barjilla*

Centre: fresh dates or *retaab*

Opposite: chickpeas or *dango*

slow braised biz'har lamb shanks

Unbelievably tender meat, slowly braised in subtle spices, falls off the bone in juicy morsels with a rich velvety sauce. As impressive as it looks, this dish is ridiculously easy to prepare and even easier to cook. The lamb shanks' flavour considerably improves by resting in the fridge overnight, making it ideal for a party - all you need to do is to reheat. Use the home-made stock recipe, pages 50- 52, or water but do not use stock cubes which are generally too salty for this much reduced and concentrated sauce. **Serves 8.**

* 600g sliced red onions
* 6 tablespoons olive oil
* 6 small and evenly sized lamb shanks
* 1 tablespoon mild *biz'har*, page 6
* 2 bruised and split cardamom pods
* 2 tablespoons cumin seeds
* 2 cinnamon sticks
* 3 cloves mashed garlic
* 2 finely chopped carrots
* 2 tablespoons fresh lemon juice
* 6 stalks of fresh parsley leaves
* 5 sprigs fresh *za'atar* or thyme
* 2 skinned, chopped tomatoes
* 1 teaspoon tomato paste
* 2 bay leaves
* 2 tablespoons *dibbs* or dark honey
* 2 1/2 litres cold water or stock, pages 50-52
* 3 tablespoons ice-cold butter, cut into cubes

1 Pour all the olive oil into a large, heavy saucepan and stir-fry the onions on a medium to low heat until they are golden brown and very crispy , about 15 minutes. Remove all of the onions with a slotted spoon, leaving behind as much of the oil as you can in the bottom of the pan; drain on a paper towel and reserve half for replacing in the dish and half for garnish. Do not wash the pan.

2 Place the lamb shanks in the same pan to brown well over a medium to high heat; season with sea salt and freshly ground black pepper. Keep turning them to brown evenly. When well browned, add the remaining ingredients in the order listed, except for the water, or stock, and the cold butter. Stir-fry the ingredients so that they brown evenly without burning. Replace half the browned onions to the pan and stir well.

3 Add cold water or stock. Bring to the boil, reduce heat and simmer gently, uncovered, for 1 hour, and thereafter partially covered for another 40 minutes, or until tender. Skim off any fat, scum or impurities that may form on the surface, and continue skimming from time to time while it cooks. Check that the meat is tender and falls off the bone. I test with a blunt knife or edge of a metal spoon. If necessary, cook for a bit longer.

4 Turn off the heat; remove the lamb shanks and place in a bowl, cover with cling wrap and set aside or leave to cool. You may prefer to strain the sauce when cool, though I don't think it is necessary; I like the rustic feel of the unstrained sauce. If making a day ahead, cover with cling wrap and refrigerate overnight. One hour before serving, remove from the fridge. Use a slotted spoon to skim off all the fat that has solidified on the surface of the sauce.

5 Bring the stock in the pan back to the boil and let it reduce, uncovered, until thickened perfectly to a sauce for serving, about 1 hour. Adjust the seasoning with additional lemon juice, sea salt and freshly ground black pepper to taste.

6 Replace and simmer the shanks in the sauce for 20 minutes. Whisk the cubes of ice-cold butter, one at a time, into the simmering stock until dissolved, around 2 minutes. Reheat the reserved browned onions in a non-stick pan without any additional oil - a quick stir-fry is all that is needed. Serve with any rice pilaf or with the recipe for chickpea rice pilaf, see overleaf, some of the sauce and the reheated browned onions piled over the shanks.

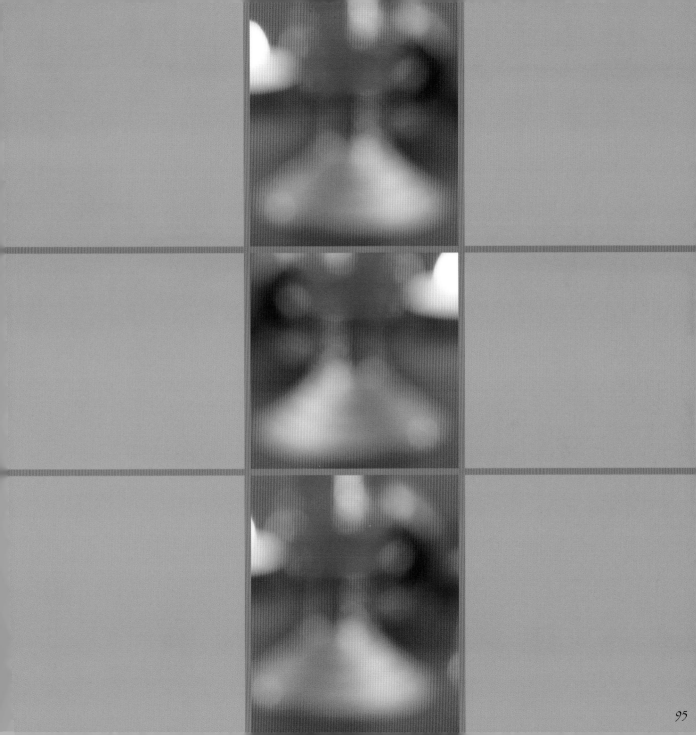

chickpea rice pilaf

Serves 3-4 as a nourishing main course along with a stew, yogurt and few side dishes, or serves 6 as an accompaniment.

* 3 cups basmati rice
* 2 tablespoons olive oil
* 1 x 400g can drained chickpeas
* 1 teaspoon powdered cumin seeds
* 2 thickly sliced medium onions
* 1 cup mixture of sultanas, almonds and pine nuts in any quantity of each that you prefer
* 2 teaspoons sea salt
* 4 cups fresh cold water or stock, pages 50-52

1 Heat 1 tablespoon of olive oil in a large non-stick, thick-bottomed pan. Add the onions and stir-fry on a low heat until browned and caramelised. Remove, drain on a paper towel and set aside.
2 Add the chickpeas, cumin, sultanas, almonds and pine nuts to the pan; season with a little of the sea salt. Stir-fry until golden brown, about 2 minutes. Remove and drain on a paper towel. Heat the remaining tablespoon of olive oil, add the rice and stir for a minute to coat with the pan's flavours. Immediately, add the water or stock, and remaining salt. Bring to the boil, uncovered, on a high heat, about 3 minutes; cover with a tightly fitting lid, reduce the heat and simmer for fifteen minutes.
3 Turn off the heat, leave partially covered to stand for 5 minutes. All the water should have been absorbed. If not, let it stand a little longer, covered, until the water is absorbed. Turn out onto a large platter, top with the reserved brown onions, sultanas, almonds and pine nuts and serve immediately, delicious with my spiked laban, page 12, and a sprinkling of fresh coriander leaves.

Sweets

Rarely served at the end of a meal, Middle Eastern desserts are irresistible mouthfuls of nutty crunch and sweet, sticky luscious creaminess. Instead, they are served as snacks with tea or coffee for mid-morning and mid-afternoon breaks, as teacakes and biscuits are in the West.

filo pastry with kashta, crushed pistachios and kalaj syrup

Crushed, crunchy pistachios are folded into luscious clouds of treble-thick cream, *kashta*, layered with crisp *filo* pastry and mouth-wateringly drizzled with caramelised rose water-flavoured *kalaj* syrup.

This dessert has all the flavour of the famous syrup-soaked sweetmeats of the Middle East but is very easy to make and impressive to serve. The *kalaj* syrup can be made ahead as it needs to be well chilled for using when assembling the dessert. If *kashta* is unavailable, whipped mascarpone or any other smooth cream cheeses are good substitutes. The *filo* can also be baked ahead, leaving the job of quick assembly before serving very easy and ideal for parties. **Makes 8-10 small *filo* pastries.**

* 1 cup granulated sugar
* 2 cups water
* 3 tablespoons rose water
* 100 ml lemon juice; 2 large lemons

* 1 packet *filo* pastry
* 1/2 cup melted ghee or butter
* 400g thick creamy *kashta* or mascarpone cream cheese
* 1 3/4 cup or 350g finely crushed pistachio nuts

1 To make the *kalaj* syrup, put the sugar in a non-stick, thick-bottomed frying pan and melt to dissolve completely without stirring the sugar. It is important to tilt the pan by the handle to move the sugar around so that it melts evenly. Within 3-4 minutes, the melted sugar will begin to take on a light golden colour; do not let it brown. Careful not to burn your hand, pour the water in from the edge of the pan. Caution: steam will rise dangerously. Once the initial burst of steam subsides, stir until the water bubbles in the pan and mixes with the sticky sugar. Let it bubble on a high heat for 12 minutes or until thickened. Add the rosewater and lemon juice. Remove from heat; when cool, pour into a bowl, cover with cling wrap and store in the fridge until needed. The syrup will keep covered in the fridge for up to 1 month.

2 Preheat oven to 190°C.

3 Follow the tips and instructions on the packaging to thaw the filo pastry. You need to work fast and handle the pastry as little as possible. Peel off one sheet; lay it down and brush very, very lightly with a little melted butter or *ghee*. Repeat with three more layers and, if the pastry becomes soft and unworkable at any point in this step, place covered in the fridge to firm up. Cut into rounds. Brush the top layer with melted *ghee* or butter and bake until golden brown and crispy, about 8-10 minutes.

4 Remove from the oven to cool and place on a paper towel to absorb the excess oil. The pastry can be prepared three or four days ahead to this stage, and stored in an airtight container at room temperature.

5 To assemble the dessert, place the *kashta* or cream cheese in a mixing bowl. If using mascarpone, whip it first. Stir in 4 tablespoons of the syrup and half a cup of pistachios and set the creamy filling aside. To serve, fill the centre of the *filo* pastry layers with some of the creamy filling. Drizzle a little of the *kalaj* syrup over the top of the *filo* pastry and sprinkle with the remaining pistachios. Serve immediately.

I am devoted to dates. Hugely versatile and wondrous, their densely concentrated texture cossets enormous nutritional value, traditionally breaking the fast during the holy month of *Ramadan*. Either given as gifts on feast days and birthdays, on their own or made into chocolates or buttery biscuits, they are always esteemed.

Opposite: dried *Damask* roses

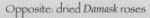

Dark, sticky and intensely nourishing, dates or their syrup, *dibbs*, flavour umm ali dessert, page 105, lamb shanks in *biz'har*, page 92, and fennel smoked *biz'har* roast *hammour* with spicy tomato sauce and couscous, page 62.

mou'hallab'ia

Smooth and sweet, *mou'hallab'ia* is creamy and chilled, a perfectly indulgent break on hot days. Scented with rose water essence, this creamy cornstarch pudding is a traditional favourite that never fails to please and it is very easy to make. I make it like pannacotta, reducing the milk and cream, and with a minimum of cornstarch.

Try making variations, such as adding 2-3 tablespoons each of lemon juice and the zest of 1 orange; or 1/2 cup each of chopped dates and desiccated coconut, topped with pistachios and a drizzle of *dibbs*; or 2 tablespoons of pomegranate syrup and 1/2 cup crushed almonds stirred into the mixture.

Serves 12 in small glass dessert bowls or 12 Moroccan tea glasses.

* 3 tablespoons or 30g cornstarch
* 3 cups or 750 ml milk
* 3 cups or 750 ml cream

* 1 cup or 200g white granulated sugar
* 3 tablespoons or 45 ml rose water
* 2-3 tablespoons or 30g crushed pistachios for garnish

1 Mix the cornstarch to a smooth milky consistency with 1 1/2 cups of milk and set aside.
2 Heat the remaining milk, cream and sugar in a very large thick-bottomed pan on a medium high heat, stirring all the time to dissolve the sugar and to bring it to a boil, about 4 minutes. Immediately reduce the heat and let it gently simmer, uncovered and without stirring, for 25 minutes.
3 Quickly whisk in the reserved cornstarch and milk mixture to prevent it from becoming lumpy. Add the rose water and additional flavourings if using. Simmer for a further 5-7 minutes, stirring all the time until the mixture thickens. Remove from the heat, let it settle for a couple of minutes, then pour into individual serving bowls or glasses; cover surface of the dessert with non-pvc cling wrap.
4 Chill for 3 hours; when ready to serve, remove the wrapping and decorate with crushed pistachios.
If using any of the variations above, top with additional lemon rind, almonds, coconut, or dates.

umm ali

Serve it at the end of a meal from a large ovenproof dish or serve it Arab-style on a tray, *fu-alla*, in individual dessert bowls with mid morning or afternoon tea or coffee. Honey-sweet dates, sultanas, sweet almonds and other nuts flavour a vanilla and rose-scented, luscious oven-hot bread and butter style pudding, which oozes rich creaminess. This is a much loved dish and a *Ramadan* favourite. I make it with baked puff pastry but you can use bread, even cornflakes, and you can have fun with this recipe throwing in whatever combinations of nuts and fruit you prefer. I like to choose honeyed, juicy, freshly harvested or *retaab* dates, or any good quality dates. I also like to intensify the date flavour with a light drizzle of *dibbs* syrup. Its delicious treacle-like taste and texture contribute to an enviable scrumptiousness. This dish freezes well and is ideal for serving at big buffet parties. **Serves 8-10.**

* 300g ready-made frozen puff pastry
* 4 cups or 1 litre milk
* 2 cups or 500 ml cream
* 1 cup or 200g sugar
* 1 vanilla pod, sliced through lengthwise
* 100 ml rose water
* 3-4 tablespoons date syrup, optional
* 1/2 cup or 125 ml double cream or *kashta*, for the topping
  the nut and fruit layers
  3-4 tablespoons or 30g roasted flaked almonds
  a handful or 12-15 cashew nuts
  3-4 teaspoons or 30g roasted pine nuts
  4 tablespoons roasted desiccated coconut
  2 handfuls or 1/2 cup of sultanas or golden raisins
  12-15 dates or roughly 150g quartered, stoned dates
  3 tablespoons or 60g pistachio nuts

1 Preheat the oven to 180°C degrees.

2 Follow the tips and instructions on the packaging to thaw and bake the pastry to a crisp golden colour. Leave to cool on a wire rack.

3 In a large saucepan, bring the milk, cream, sugar and the vanilla pod to the boil. Reduce the heat and let it simmer for 40 minutes to thicken slightly. Stir in the rose water, remove from the heat and set aside.

4 Dry-roast the almonds, cashew nuts and pine nuts in a non-stick frying pan for 1-2 minutes; add the coconut and let the mixture brown carefully to a roasted golden colour, around 4 minutes on a medium to low heat, stirring all the time. Transfer to a mixing bowl and set aside to cool. When cool, add all the remaining ingredients for the nut and fruit layers and mix to combine well.

5 Remove the vanilla pod from the milk, leaving behind its tiny seeds that speckle the flavoured milk. Put a shallow layer of the milk into the bottom of an ovenproof tart dish or bowl. Break or cut the pastry into large pieces and place a third of them to cover the milk layer. Sprinkle over a third of the nut and fruit mixture and, if using, a drizzle of the *dibbs*. Repeat the layering: milk - pastry - nuts and fruits, using up all the ingredients until the bowl is two-thirds full and topping with a final layer of pastry. You can prepare the dessert a day ahead up to the end of this stage: cover with cling wrap and leave the milk to soak into the pastry and all the nuts. When cool place in the fridge or freezer. When needed, bring to room temperature, about 30 minutes or at least 4 hours if frozen.

6 Preheat the oven to 180°C.

7 Pour the double cream to cover the surface of the dessert and bake. It should take around 35 minutes for the cream to brown lightly and for the dessert to cook. Serve immediately, or keep warm and serve within 30 minutes or the cream on the surface will be re-absorbed into the dessert, spoiling its pretty appearance and lusciously velvet texture.

desert transport over subkah and sands
1977

Making a note of…

* While airfreight delivers the world's ingredients to local markets around the world, I still search for organic, home-grown, glistening fresh, sun-ripened deep colours, and vibrant scented aromas in herbs and raw ingredients. Make it your business to find out where and who grew the food or raised the stock, and select only the best seasonal ingredients.

* Many of my recipes require marinades which happily need only your forward planning and not your valuable time. I always use a non-pvc cling wrap to cover the bowl in which the meat or fish is marinated and I suggest that you keep it refrigerated unless the recipe directs otherwise.

* All spices are whole where possible and then powdered, bruised or crushed. If you don't have a mill shop nearby, a pestle and mortar, coffee grinder or small, strong blender will grind whole spices to a powder efficiently.

* I stir-fry the ingredients using careful, measured amounts of olive oil. Ghee is used only as flavouring. Only use extra virgin olive oil for salad dressings or when specifically required. For cooking, use olive oil.

* Caution for blending hot liquids: cool slightly and blend directly in the pan with a stick blender; it is safer than transferring hot soup to an enclosed blender, where it can 'explode' when the blender is switched on.

* To skin and seed tomatoes, boil a large pan of fresh water. Cut an 'x' on each tomato at the opposite end to the stalk. Put all the tomatoes in the boiling water and simmer for 3-4 minutes. For smaller quantities, simply pour boiling water over the tomatoes and leave to stand for 5 minutes. Remove with a slotted spoon to a colander and rinse under cold water; transfer to a bowl. When cool enough to handle, peel, cut in half and seed them.

* Heavy saucepans are thick-bottomed. Use preferably non-stick ones or cast-iron casseroles to brown food without burning. If you don't already have them, please consider investing in them. Without them, many of these recipes, especially the stove-top cooked biryani-style rice pilafs, would burn.

* Suggested times are guidelines only. Recipe results vary according to pot size and thickness and actual heat temperatures applied.

I use a cup = 250 ml; 4 cups = 1 litre; 1 tablespoon =15 ml; and 1 teaspoon = 5 ml measurements.

Arabic sweets make for excellent desserts as well, perfumed with rose petal water or syrup, crunchy with pistachio and almonds, sticky with dates and caramelised milk reductions, fragrant with vanilla. Serve them, Arab-style, on a large metal platter or tray, *fu'alla*, together with freshly brewed cardamon coffee or herbed tea, as well as generously filled bowls of chocolates, dates and sliced fruit.

desert sunset, near Lahbab 1977

www.foodstyling.ae

The author, Jessie Kirkness Parker, a fourth generation South African, first came to the United Arab Emirates in the 1970s, when many of the photographs in this book were taken.

Twenty five years as a freelance TV and still food stylist, and for many years as the contributing food editor and food writer for the Gulf News has given her a special insight into Middle Eastern customs and traditions. A Taste of Arabia, her first book, a best seller in the English version is now available in Arabic.

Jessie is a flavour consultant and designer developing recipes, menus and cookery books and project manages food styling for television and still photography. She regularly contributes to leading Middle East newspapers. Her work takes her on extensive travels around the world researching food and travel features. Jessie divides her time between their farmhouse in France and the Middle East where she lives with her husband, Keith. Her two girls live in the United Kingdom and the States.

Acknowledgements

This book could not have been accomplished without the support of the energetic team at Jerboa Books – the inspirational Isobel Abulhoul, the indefatigable publishing editor Jane Hodges, the hugely talented artist Lina Abouljoud and the meticulous Tensingh.

To my recipe editor, Joan Scott-Minter, who, in picking up my manuscript, identified my 'voice', and spent hours working out how to make the sentences in my recipes acceptable without losing it. Bless you.

To Trevor Vaughan, who suffered me as a demanding client, giving me total freedom to art direct each recipe design in the way I have always wanted to style Middle Eastern food and table tops – a huge thank you for your superb lighting and photography.

To Joan, Gina, Emily and Keith for their thorough attention to detail in the enormous task of triple-testing the recipes, thank you.

To my precious friends, women who have nurtured me and made me laugh when times were tough, many *salaams* and grateful thanks.

To my treasured girls, who obligingly tasted every strange and wonderful food in many countries as they grew up, and for the joy of mealtimes with them - darlings, thank you.

Finally, to my husband Keith for the richness of many years of inspiration and support in my travels and investigative cooking, and for being my chief taster when really he would have preferred a *braai* – thank you.

Cover: Big Red, Dubai-Hatta Road
1977
Between the Hajar Mountains and
the great Rub Al Khali Desert
Picture by Keith Parker

Damask roses